NEW DIRECTIONS FOR EVALUATION
A Publication of the American Evaluation Association

Lois-ellin G. Datta, *Datta Analysis*
EDITOR-IN-CHIEF

Evaluation and Auditing: Prospects for Convergence

Carl Wisler
Wisler Associates

EDITOR

Number 71, Fall 1996

JOSSEY-BASS PUBLISHERS
San Francisco

EVALUATION AND AUDITING: PROSPECTS FOR CONVERGENCE
Carl Wisler (ed.)
New Directions for Evaluation, no. 71
Lois-ellin G. Datta, Editor-in-Chief

Microfilm copies of issues and articles are available in 16mm and 35mm, as well as microfiche in 105mm, through University Microfilms Inc., 300 North Zeeb Road, Ann Arbor, Michigan 48106-1346.

ISSN 0164-7989   ISBN 0-7879-9887-7

NEW DIRECTIONS FOR EVALUATION is part of The Jossey-Bass Education Series and is published quarterly by Jossey-Bass Inc., Publishers, 350 Sansome Street, San Francisco, California 94104-1342.

Subscriptions cost $61.00 for individuals and $96.00 for institutions, agencies, and libraries.

EDITORIAL CORRESPONDENCE should be addressed to the Editor-in-Chief, Lois-ellin G. Datta, P.O. Box 383768, Waikoloa, HI 96738.

TCF Manufactured in the United States of America on Lyons Falls Pathfinder Tradebook. This paper is acid-free and 100 percent totally chlorine-free.

EDITORIAL POLICY AND PROCEDURES

NEW DIRECTIONS FOR EVALUATION, a quarterly sourcebook, is an official publication of the American Evaluation Association. The journal publishes empirical, methodological, and theoretical works on all aspects of evaluation and related fields. Substantive areas may include any program, field, or issue with which evaluation is concerned, such as government performance, tax policy, energy, environment, mental health, education, job training, medicine, and public health. Also included are such topics as product evaluation, personnel evaluation, policy analysis, and technology assessment. In all cases, the focus on evaluation is more important than the substantive topics. We are particularly interested in encouraging a diversity of evaluation perspectives and experiences and in expanding the boundaries of our field beyond the evaluation of social programs.

The editors do not consider or publish unsolicited single manuscripts. Each issue of the journal is devoted to a single topic, with contributions solicited, organized, reviewed, and edited by a guest editor. Issues may take any of several forms, such as a series of related chapters, a debate, or a long article followed by brief critical commentaries. In all cases, the proposals must follow a specific format, which can be obtained from the editor-in-chief. These proposals are sent to members of the editorial board and to relevant substantive experts for peer review. The process may result in acceptance, a recommendation to revise and resubmit, or rejection. However, the editors are committed to working constructively with potential guest editors to help them develop acceptable proposals.

Lois-ellin G. Datta, Editor-in-Chief
P.O. Box 383768
Waikoloa, HI 96738

Jennifer C. Greene, Associate Editor
Department of Human Service Studies
Cornell University
Ithaca, NY 14853-4401

Gary Henry, Associate Editor
Public Administration and Urban Studies
Georgia State University
Atlanta, GA 30302-4039

CONTENTS

EDITOR'S NOTES

During the last several decades, the disciplines of evaluation and auditing have each gone through substantial change. The purpose of this volume is not to explore all the reasons and consequences associated with such change, but to focus on the extent to which audit and evaluation have converged on similar procedures and organizational structures and on the extent to which they have remained different. An effort has been made to understand and describe the issues from both evaluation and auditing perspectives.

Both evaluation and auditing claim to help decision makers by providing them with systematic and credible information that can be useful in the creation, management, oversight, change, and occasionally abolishment of programs. Yet despite considerable overlap in objectives, subject matter, and clients, auditing and evaluation have until recently functioned largely in isolation from one another. The literature of each discipline scarcely recognizes the existence of the other. Academic preparation of auditors and evaluators could hardly be more different. Organizationally, the two activities have traditionally been separate. The practitioners have difficulty communicating with one another not only because of differences in vocabulary but also because of some important differences in mind-set. Will auditing and evaluation persist as distinctive services to decision makers or is there a possibility of a merge or blend of the two activities?

Differences between auditing and evaluation are rooted in the older professions from which they emerged. Auditing evolved from financial accounting and so makes much use of concepts like verification, internal controls, and good management practice. Evaluation emerged from the sciences, especially social science, and so has tended to carry with it the trappings of measurement, probability sampling, and experimentation. The authors represented in this volume make frequent reference to the conceptual underpinnings of the two disciplines when they point out how auditing and evaluation are different.

One way to get a quick sense of some differences between auditing and evaluation is to consider the kinds of questions for which the two fields have tried to provide answers. Three categories of questions are especially useful for comparing auditing and evaluation: descriptive, normative, and cause-and-effect (Wisler, 1984a, 1984b). These categories are explicitly or implicitly referred to any number of times in the following chapters.

Program evaluation has always given much attention to cause-and-effect questions, especially ones about the overall impact of a program. The answer to an impact question is usually formulated as the difference between an outcome observed after a program has been in operation with the outcome that would have been observed in the absence of the program. Evaluation clients also seek the answers to descriptive questions—ones that do not compare two conditions but simply describe a state of the world. Common examples include questions about the societal needs, the setting in which a program operates, or the way a program was implemented.

Auditing has traditionally focused on normative questions for which the answer compares "what is" with "what should be." Seldom do auditors seek answers to descriptive questions nor do they often consider cause-and-effect questions, at least in the sense that evaluators understand that term.

One of the most interesting differences in disciplinary perspective is the contrast between program audit, which usually starts with a normative question, and impact evaluation, which focuses on cause and effect. A brief overview of these two forms of inquiry is illuminating because practitioners from each discipline claim that their respective approaches address the issue of program effectiveness. However, the similarity seems to end there. Methodologically, they are different because in fact they address two distinct questions about program effectiveness. Although the two methodological approaches can be distinguished easily, it is probable that most clients, and at least some practitioners as well, do not fully appreciate the important differences.

As defined by the Comptroller General of the United States (1994, p. 14), *performance audit* is "an objective and systematic examination of evidence . . . of the performance of a government organization, program, activity, or function in order to provide information to improve public accountability and facilitate decision-making." A *program audit* is a subcategory of a performance audit for which one objective (of three) is to determine "the extent to which the desired results or benefits established by the legislature or other authorizing body are being achieved." This application of program audit provides an interesting contrast with impact evaluation. (The scope of auditing is broad, of course, and the practitioners may employ objectives and methodologies different from those reviewed here. The notion of value-for-money audits, used in many countries, is similar to the concept of performance auditing.)

Schandl (1978, p. 4) says "auditing is a human evaluation process to establish the adherence to certain norms, resulting in an opinion (or judgment)." Herbert (1979) describes developments at the U.S. General Accounting Office in the 1960s that led to a prescription for management and program audits; those prescriptions are comparable to the general concept set forth by Schandl regarding how to undertake management and program audits. The central idea in a program audit is to compare "what is" with "what should be" (Comptroller General of the United States, 1979 [1974]). This notion seems to flow from earlier forms of auditing in which generally accepted accounting practices or, more broadly, generally accepted management practices played key roles. The methodology was to establish a standard generally accepted management practice, for example, and to compare that standard with actual program practice. Any discovery of a serious discrepancy would be regarded as a deficiency and lead to a negative audit report.

In moving to broader issues of program effectiveness, auditors took along the normative question. To conduct a program audit, it was therefore necessary to identify one or more specific program objectives to play the role of "what should be." Such objectives might come from legislation, regulations, declarations of intent by program managers, and so on. Actual program performance, determined empirically, provided the "what is" component. And program effect was defined as the difference between the program objective and actual performance. (In auditing, an effect is sometimes defined differently to mean the consequences of a discrepancy. For example, if a program to improve water quality showed a shortfall in the achievement of water purity standards, the effects might be greater incidence of disease, lost time at work due to illness, and so on.)

The audit approach to program effectiveness is in the spirit of the strategy advocated in the problem-solving literature as exemplified by Kepner and Tregoe (1976). It is also very much in the mode of objectives-oriented evaluation approaches (see Chapter 5 of Worthen and Sanders, 1987) sometimes used with educational programs—and especially of the version called discrepancy evaluation (Provus, 1971). It does not correspond, however, to the conventional notion of impact evaluation.

Program impact evaluation stems from the experimental design used in a number of sciences wherein comparisons are made between outcomes associated with randomly assigned treatment and control groups. In evaluation, the methodology is generally understood not to require random assignment but to extend to other approaches that permit comparisons between what happened in the presence of the program and what would have happened in the absence of the program. Such quasi-experimental designs are prominent in evaluation as ways to answer impact questions (Cook and Campbell, 1979). (Auditors and others new to the evaluation literature have to contend with the variety of terms that may be used interchangeably with impact evaluation, most notably impact assessment, impact analysis, and program effectiveness evaluation.)

The two questions posed by auditors and evaluators about program effectiveness can, and generally will, lead to quite different conclusions about the performance of a program. Both conclusions may be correct—they are just answers to different questions. Unfortunately, because of the language used, the unwary may perceive the questions to be the same.

The foregoing comparison of program audit and impact evaluation illustrates the purpose of this volume, not to give a full-featured account of the heartlands of evaluation and auditing, but more to focus on the territory where they come together. The authors of the five chapters of this volume have all been in positions to survey the terrain that is roamed both by bands of evaluators and of auditors, and they offer their views on the jointly occupied territory along with occasional references to the heartlands. Earlier versions of the chapters were presented at a session of the International Evaluation Conference held in Vancouver, British Columbia, November 1–5, 1995.

Stan Divorski, from his vantage point with the Office of the Auditor General in Canada, sets forth five key dimensions that he finds distinguish the mind-sets of evaluators from auditors. Roger Brooks uses his perspective in the

Minnesota Office of Legislative Auditor to consider the extent to which the auditing and evaluation cultures have been blended, or at least have that potential if blending is desired. Christopher Pollitt and Hilkka Summa bring their experiences with audit institutions in the United Kingdom and Finland, respectively, to bear in comparing the ways in which auditors and evaluators approach similar tasks. Frans L. Leeuw from the Netherlands Court of Audit focuses on the contributions of evaluators and auditors to the improvement of public sector performance and, in so doing, draws attention to a slice of the international literature comparing the two fields. Finally, Eleanor Chelimsky, formerly of the U.S. General Accounting Office, highlights the conclusions of the other authors, based on their conference papers, and offers her own views on the pros and cons of integrating auditing and evaluation or keeping them as separate services to decision makers.

Collectively, the authors point out many similarities and differences between auditing and evaluation. Indeed, there is such variety in the observations that it is difficult to categorize them and gauge their importance. If, as seems to be the case, evaluation and auditing are moving closer together, what are the differences that seem most likely to hold them apart? Readers may wish to consider the following three themes and conjectures as they read this volume.

The inclination of auditors toward normative questions and of evaluators toward descriptive and impact questions. The difference is rooted in the history of the disciplines and in the educational preparation of the practitioners. Although examples of crossover between the disciplines can be cited, a broad-scale mix of the approaches seems likely to take a long time, if it ever occurs.

Independence versus collaboration with the subjects of audit and evaluation. Auditors have attached great importance to their independence from both client and auditee, while evaluators have tended to work more closely with their clients and to move toward yet greater collaboration with evaluees. Even if the tenets of fourth-generation evaluation are not adopted by most evaluators, mainstream evaluators seem unlikely to return to the extremes of scientific detachment that once prevailed. The two disciplines therefore seem destined to be some distance apart on the scale of independence.

Differences in the degree to which auditing and evaluation have become routinized government operations. The role of auditing in government activities has been generally acknowledged with legislative mandates, clearly identified clients, and organizational permanence. The shorter history of public program evaluation reveals less widespread acceptance, more variability and multiplicity of clients, and considerable fluctuation in fortune over the short term. The repercussions of these differences on achievements of the two disciplines (in terms of program improvements, new legislation, and so on) may be hard to sort out, but in the case of evaluation, one wonders how long the shakedown cruise will last and how, or if, a greater stability will be achieved. A continued convergence of evaluation and auditing might be a course toward a higher-quality, more steadfast service to decision makers.

References

Comptroller General of the United States. "Report Manual." As adapted in L. Herbert, *Auditing the Performance of Management*. Belmont, Calif.: Lifetime Learning, 1979. (Originally published 1974.)

Comptroller General of the United States. *Government Auditing Standards, 1994 Revision*. Washington, D.C.: U.S. General Accounting Office, 1994.

Cook, T. D., and Campbell, D. T. *Quasi-Experimentation*. Skokie, Ill.: Rand McNally, 1979.

Herbert, L. *Auditing the Performance of Management*. Belmont, Calif.: Lifetime Learning, 1979.

Kepner, C. H., and Tregoe, B. B. *The Rational Manager*. (2nd ed.). Princeton, N.J.: Kepner-Tregoe, 1976.

Provus, M. M. *Discrepancy Evaluation*. Berkeley, Calif.: McCutchan, 1971.

Schandl, C. W. *Theory of Auditing*. Houston, Tex.: Scholars, 1978.

Wisler, C. E. "Topics in Evaluation." *GAO Review*, 1984a, 19–1.

Wisler, C. E. "Topics in Evaluation." *GAO Review*, 1984b, 19–3.

Worthen, B. R., and Sanders, J. R. *Educational Evaluation*. New York: Longman, 1987.

CARL WISLER is an evaluation consultant with Wisler Associates in Mitchellville, Maryland.

Although audits and evaluations may have similar characteristics,
the perspectives of auditors and evaluators can be quite different.
These differing perspectives are reflected in their respective treatments
of program impacts.

Differences in the Approaches of Auditors and Evaluators to the Examination of Government Policies and Programs

Stan Divorski

On any given dimension, the extent to which audit and evaluation differ is largely a matter of degree. Any characteristic that can apply to audits will also apply to some evaluations, somewhere, sometime. Any distinguishing characteristic of evaluations probably can be found to apply to some audit. Overall, however, audits and evaluations can be very different.

This chapter attempts to describe the perspective, the mind-set, that auditors bring to the examination of programs, so as to illustrate how different the perspectives of auditors and evaluators can be. Although this perspective has its origins in the requirements of financial auditing, the focus here is on value-for-money auditing, which includes the examination of program activities, as well as of management systems and procedures for controlling these activities.

Five key dimensions distinguish this mind-set from that of evaluators. In general, auditors:

- Make a judgment as to how adequate or inadequate are the matters examined.
- Make this judgment against a preestablished set of criteria.
- Focus on management systems and procedures for controlling program activities rather than on the program activities themselves.

The views expressed in this chapter are those of the author and should not be construed as representing those of the Auditor General of Canada.

- May avoid commenting on substantive government policies.
- View information on program results (when considered at all) as evidence of other matters, rather than as an end in itself.

Judging Against Pre-Established Criteria

The mandate for an auditor's work requires a judgment about the adequacy of the matters examined. Such judgment is based on a comparison of the results of the examination against a set of criteria, or expectations, that the auditor may draw from a variety of sources, including previous audits and professional standards or guidelines.

For example, in reporting an audit of *The Control and Clean-up of Freshwater Pollution,* the Auditor General of Canada stated that it "expected to find that the various federal components of action plans were coordinated and that the means were in place to handle interdepartmental conflicts over policy, planning and funding as action plans are implemented" (1993b, p. 370). In addition to general criteria of this nature, an auditor may establish more specific subcriteria.

The way in which a judgment is reached and expressed depends upon the assignment the auditor receives. The auditor may reach a judgment after examining directly the matters at hand or after examining the reliability of management's assertions. At times the two approaches may be combined. The choice of approach may be imposed by the auditor, the client, or, in the case of a legislated mandate, by law.

An interesting example of the audit of periodic financial statements is that recommended by the Canadian Comprehensive Auditing Foundation (CCAF) for reporting on effectiveness (1987). The CCAF recommends that management make representations (that is, that they provide information about effectiveness in their organizations), and that auditors provide opinions on the fairness of those representations. Rather than define effectiveness, the CCAF sets out twelve attributes of effectiveness against which managers are expected to report:

1. Management direction (including clarity of objectives)
2. Continued relevance of a program
3. Appropriateness of program design
4. Achievement of intended results
5. Satisfaction of clients or stakeholders
6. Secondary impacts
7. Costs and productivity
8. Responsiveness to changed circumstances
9. Financial results
10. The extent to which the organization provides an appropriate work environment for its employees
11. Safeguarding of assets
12. Monitoring and reporting of performance

The conditions on an audit engagement may also specify how the auditor is to report the judgment. In *exception reporting,* the auditor is required to report any deficiencies; that is, situations that did not meet these criteria. Canada's Auditor General Act, Section 7(2), gives such a mandate:

Each report of the Auditor General under subsection (1) shall call attention to anything that he [*sic*] considers to be of significance and of a nature that should be brought to the attention of the House of Commons, including any cases in which he has observed that

(a) accounts have not been faithfully and properly maintained or public money has not been fully accounted for or paid, where so required by law, into the consolidated revenue fund;

(b) essential records have not been maintained or the rules and procedures applied have been insufficient to safeguard and control public property, to secure an effective check on the assessment, collection and proper allocation of the revenue and to ensure that expenditures have been made only as authorized;

(c) money has been expended other than for purposes for which it was appropriated by Parliament;

(d) money has been expended without due regard to economy or efficiency;

(e) satisfactory procedures have not been established to measure and report the effectiveness of programs, where such procedures could appropriately and reasonably be implemented; or

(f) money has been expended without due regard to the environmental effects of those expenditures in the context of sustainable development.

For example, in the audit of *The Control and Clean-up of Freshwater Pollution* described earlier, the auditor reported instances of poor coordination and unresolved conflicts: "This difference in departmental objectives and program funding led to coordination problems. Although the two departments agreed to provide for a management structure to coordinate their respective programs, [the structure] proved to be ineffective" (1993b, p. 374).

Alternatively, an auditor may be required to report on the level of comfort or *assurance* that a third party can have regarding the management of the program. The CCAF model for effectiveness auditing is one example of an assurance engagement. In this instance, the auditor provides assurance regarding management representations as to the matters at hand. Another example of an assurance mandate is provided in Part X of Canada's Financial Administration Act (1991), bearing on the responsibilities of Crown Corporations. Subsection 138(1) of the act requires corporations to engage an auditor to undertake a special examination, in which the auditor is required to "determine if the systems and practices referred to in paragraph 131(1)(b) were, in the period under examination, maintained in a manner that provided reasonable assurance that they met the requirements of paragraphs 131(2)(a) and (c)."

Subsection 131(2) clarifies that "The books, records, systems and practices referred to in subsection (1) shall be kept and maintained in such manner as will provide reasonable assurance that . . . (c) the financial, human and physical resources of the corporation and each subsidiary are managed economically and efficiently and the operations of the corporation and each subsidiary are carried out effectively." In this instance, the inability to find an exception from the positive expectation would be considered a judgment in confirmation of it.

In assurance engagements, a positive judgment is reached and reported with great care because (1) available methods may be incorrectly applied or not foolproof, and (2) there may be an undetected case that constitutes an important variation from the expectations established.

Focus on Management

The core business of an audit is the examination of management controls over expenditure, including whether or not management has in place the systems and procedures necessary to ensure that expenditures are made with due regard to economy and efficiency and in compliance with existing regulations or policies. Evaluation rarely intrudes into these areas. The distinction between audit and evaluation has become blurred, however, through increasing attention by audit to management control over results, including program effects, as an indication of good financial management and control.

This change has been reinforced by trends in government to decrease the emphasis on formal controls and increase the delegation of authority, accompanied by a greater need for accountability for results on the part of managers.

The mandate for audits of Crown Corporations under Canada's Financial Administration Act (1991) reflects this focus on management, as it requires attention to management systems and practices. Of particular significance to a comparison of auditors and evaluators, the act specifically requires the auditor to consider management control over the effectiveness of program operations.

The approach recommended by the Canadian Comprehensive Auditing Foundation (CCAF) for auditing effectiveness also reflects the auditor's focus on improving management. The CCAF notes that "The decision to emphasize management representations reflects the reporting obligations of managers, the needs of governing bodies, and their mutual desire for better management" (1991, p. 9).

The focus on management issues rather than outcomes per se is reflected in the CCAF's twelve attributes of effectiveness, which include such matters as managers' responsibility for costs and productivity, responsiveness to changed circumstances, provision of an appropriate working environment, and so on.

Restrictions on the Scope of Audit

Under the CCAF approach, the auditor is potentially limited in the scope of the investigation by the information that the manager chooses to report.

There may be other, more formal restrictions on the scope of audit work. This is especially likely to apply to the examination of major government policies. For example, with regard to the special examination of Crown Corporations, Section 145 of Canada's Financial Administration Act specifies, "Nothing in this Part or the regulations shall be construed as authorizing the examiner of a Crown corporation to express any opinion on the merits of matters of policy, including the merits of . . . (c) any business or policy decision of the corporation or of the Government of Canada."

Other examples are provided by the Swedish National Audit Office (1995, p. 8) and the Australian National Audit Office (1995, p. 1.3), whose mandates specifically exclude comment on government policy.

When Auditors Examine Results

To this point, I have argued that auditors are more likely than evaluators to focus on management systems and procedures and to face restrictions on their freedom to comment on policy. I have also pointed out that the mandate of auditors frequently includes effectiveness. It is in the area of examining effectiveness that the distinction between audit and evaluation is least clear, although reducing to two basic issues. The first is the focus of effectiveness work for each. The second is the reasons why auditors and evaluators tackle issues of program effectiveness.

The model for results-based audit depicted in Table 1.1 illustrates the possible foci for effectiveness work.

The model locates results measurement of government programs along two dimensions: the level of results measured and the level of program analyzed. With regard to the program level, a distinction is made between the results of management systems and procedures and the results of program activities. Systems and procedures include such matters as planning, management information systems, and procedures for detecting, recording, and collecting overpayments to program clientele. Program evaluation itself is viewed as a management control over program effectiveness. The levels of results identified include economy and efficiency, the achievement of intermediate program objectives, and the achievement of overall program objectives.

Thus a results-based audit could potentially examine the efficiency of program activities, the extent to which these activities further intermediate program objectives, or the extent to which they further the achievement of overall program objectives. Audits may also examine the effect of management controls on efficiency or the achievement of intermediate or ultimate program objectives.

A few examples will help illustrate the model. In 1993, the Office of the Auditor General examined management controls over pension benefit payments. The audit concluded that the systems and procedures in place for the recording, control, and collection of overpayments fell far short of meeting minimum standards for such accounts (1993d, p. 486). In discussing the importance of these deficiencies, the audit observed that overpayments represented

Table 1.1. A Model for the Focus of Results-Based Audits

		Level of Results Measured	
Program Level Audited	*Economy and Efficiency*	*Achievement of Intermediate Objectives*	*Achievement of Program Objectives*
Program activities	Costs of certain search and rescue vessels exceed benefits. 1992b Paragraph 8.53	Potential for enduring benefits of foreign economic and social development projects less than anticipated because self-sustainability was not assured in the majority of projects. 1993a Paragraphs 12.87–12.88	Lower than expected reduction in number of program participants dependent on fishery. 1993c Paragraphs 15.84–15.86, 15.93
Systems and procedures	Overpayments under pension plans for seniors increase administrative cost of program delivery. 1993d Paragraphs 18.69–18.70	Weaknesses in the monitoring, review, and control systems contributed to an increase of payments in situations where they were without foundation. 1992a Paragraph 7.64	Payments designed to permit sur- plus employees to quit immediately exceeded person-year reductions in staff. 1992a Paragraph 7.32

Note: All citations are to Auditor General of Canada reports of the indicated dates.

0.5 percent of total program payments, increasing the administrative cost of program delivery by more than 50 percent. The observation does not bear on the potential contribution that management controls may make to program effectiveness, but rather on their effects on the costs of program delivery.

By comparison, an audit of Search and Rescue examined the relative efficiency of program activities, specifically the types of rescue vessels employed. The audit concluded that the largest class of vessels were the most costly and had not been critical to saving any lives during the period audited (1992b, p. 225).

Management systems and controls may also have an impact on the achievement of program objectives. In 1992, the Auditor General of Canada reported on a program of payments to government employees scheduled to be laid off. The payments were expected to permit employees who so desired to quit immediately if there was no work to be performed and to save costs of employee benefits, retraining, and finding a job (1992a, p. 189). The audit observed that the number of payments, in all years except one, had consistently exceeded the reduction in person years (p. 194). Moreover, the auditors concluded that the situation was one indicator of problems in the administration of the policy, pointing to such matters as inadequate planning, no appropriate management framework, and the failure of senior management to provide leadership direction and support (p. 196).

Results as Evidence of Management Deficiencies

As noted earlier, the core business of audit is the examination of management controls over expenditure management. It is therefore the bottom row of Table 1.1 where audits will commonly be found. Economy and efficiency of program operations, the left-hand column of Table 1.1, is also a common matter for attention by audit. However, control over results as an indication of good financial management and control has also become an audit concern, leading to increased attention to the contribution of program operations to intermediate and overall program objectives. The result is illustrated by the cases cited in Table 1.1. No area of effectiveness is exempt from attention by audit.

It is in attention to the contribution of program activities to intermediate and ultimate program objectives where the functions of audit and evaluation become most difficult to distinguish. In principle, it is in the examination of activities in relationship to intermediate program objectives where the two may be most likely to overlap, but the central focus is substantially different. For an auditor, problems with the effectiveness of program activities is of interest as an indication of the importance of deficiencies in program management. The auditor will do sufficient work to assess whether program effectiveness is at risk, before turning attention to the management factors that should enable managers to gain control over program results. This may involve relying on evaluations conducted by program management, synthesizing the findings of evaluations of similar programs in other jurisdictions, and, as a last resort, conducting measurement and analyses of program impacts.

For an auditor, the attribution of impacts to program activities is less important than in the classic social scientific model of evaluation. In the social science–based model, the rigorous pursuit of the causal link between the program and its outcomes is the main focus. For an auditor, it is sufficient to determine that results *may* be inadequate, whatever the cause. If results appear to be positive, there is no deficiency to report and no need to elaborate the causal chain.

If there are problems with results, the search is on for deficiencies in practices that may have impeded management from detecting and solving the problem or for related areas of program weakness. However, this search does not necessarily involve exploration of the causal chain, for the auditor's job is not to solve management's problems but to identify that there is a problem to be solved and the areas that may be involved. In fact, it may be sufficient for an auditor to point out that management has done little to measure program effectiveness.

This lack of attention to a rigorous exploration of the causal chain may puzzle evaluators. The answer to the puzzle is that for an auditor, information on results provides evidence of other matters and is not an end in itself.

References

Auditor General of Canada. "Payments to Employees Under the Work Force Adjustment Policy." In *Report of the Auditor General of Canada.* Ottawa: Minister of Public Works and Government Services Canada, 1992a.

Auditor General of Canada. "Search and Rescue." In *Report of the Auditor General of Canada.* Ottawa: Minister of Public Works and Government Services Canada, 1992b.

Auditor General of Canada. "CIDA—Bilateral Economic and Social Development Programs." In *Report of the Auditor General of Canada.* Ottawa: Minister of Public Works and Government Services Canada, 1993a.

Auditor General of Canada. "Department of the Environment—The Control and Clean-Up of Freshwater Pollution." In *Report of the Auditor General of Canada.* Ottawa: Minister of Public Works and Government Services Canada, 1993b.

Auditor General of Canada. "Department of Fisheries and Oceans—Northern Cod Adjustment and Recovery Program." In *Report of the Auditor General of Canada.* Ottawa: Minister of Public Works and Government Services Canada, 1993c.

Auditor General of Canada. "Department of National Health and Welfare—Programs for Seniors." In *Report of the Auditor General of Canada.* Ottawa: Minister of Public Works and Government Services Canada, 1993d.

Australian National Audit Office. *Performance Auditing.* Canberra: Australian National Audit Office, 1995.

Canada Financial Administration Act. R.S. 1985, c. F–11, S. 1. Ottawa: Government of Canada, 1991.

Canadian Comprehensive Auditing Foundation. *Effectiveness Reporting and Auditing in the Public Sector. Summary Report.* Ottawa: Canadian Comprehensive Auditing Foundation, 1987.

Swedish National Audit Office. *Performance Auditing at the Swedish National Audit Office.* Stockholm: Swedish National Audit Office, 1995.

STAN DIVORSKI is a director with the Office of the Auditor General, Canada, where he has conducted governmentwide audits of evaluation in the Canadian federal government.

The divisions between traditional auditors and program evaluators, while real, are declining. The approaches and methods used by the two are becoming blended in the context of state legislative auditing and evaluation, where the two work side by side and respond to the singular demands of a unique client.

Blending Two Cultures: State Legislative Auditing and Evaluation

Roger A. Brooks

More than thirty-five years ago, the British writer C. P. Snow (1959) observed that Western intellectuals in the twentieth century were divided into two cultures—one of humanistic discourse and one of scientific reason. Each group of thinkers had developed concepts, linguistic conventions, and values that were so different from each other as to be almost mutually unintelligible. In the terminology of a later writer (Kuhn, 1962), society had evolved two separate *paradigms* that guided contemporary thought. The result was not only a fractured life of the mind, but a divided society in which people looked at issues in very different ways.

A similar analogy may apply to the divisions between auditors and evaluators plying their trades in the realm of contemporary public policy and management. The two groups often operate in the same organizations and sometimes perform similar functions on behalf of their clients.

But each group draws upon a unique intellectual tradition, operates according to a particular set of assumptions, takes a different approach to examining performance, and employs a distinctive vocabulary in its work. Auditors focus on issues like an organization's internal controls, developing standardized research methodologies that evaluators refer to somewhat pejoratively as *cookbook* methods. Evaluators, on the other hand, have no fixed methodologies or evaluative criteria, have developed their own specialized language, and, true to their social scientific roots, do not always arrive at definitive, convincing conclusions. Auditors and evaluators often work side by side, but they are often puzzled by each other's approach.

But is the two cultures analogy fair? Is there a deep gulf dividing auditors and evaluators? If so, what are the prospects for bridging the gulf? This chapter argues that the divisions between auditors and evaluators are real enough, but declining. Within the arena of state legislative program evaluation and auditing, the gulf between the two has narrowed and a new blended approach has evolved, shaped largely by the demands of state legislatures. The blended approach draws upon the unique aspects of auditing and evaluating and is successful with state legislatures because it responds to client needs.

Comparing Auditing and Evaluation

Auditing and evaluation arise from completely different traditions. Emerging from the realm of accounting, auditing emphasizes the process of checking or verifying records to find out whether they are consistent with agreed-upon standards. This is a matter of comparing observed performance to accepted criteria—in other words, comparing "what is" to "what should be"—so as to arrive at conclusions about the appropriateness of a practice. The end result is an *opinion* about whether the observed performance is consistent with accepted norms.

Audit opinions typically note deviations from expectations. This approach, called *exception reporting,* emphasizes performance that falls short of standards. A "clean" audit opinion asserts that no shortcomings were found, but, interestingly, it does not testify that there were no problems.

Arising as a profession in the midst of commercial and industrial development in nineteenth-century Britain, auditing gained stature as the need for verifiably accurate and dependable financial records grew. Auditors' work lent credibility to the growing capitalist infrastructure of the West. Auditors' opinions carried weight because of their technical craftsmanship and because auditors were outsiders.

Government auditing also developed in the nineteenth century. By the end of the century, most governments had acquired the services of auditors in an effort to assure that public money was fully accounted for and handled appropriately. After the Civil War, many states employed examiners to check records and verify accounts. Some elected state auditors to manage state resources and oversee public accounts. In 1921, the federal government created the U.S. General Accounting Office to oversee federal expenditures.

Today, auditing is a more complicated business. It has become highly professionalized through numerous associations that have spawned auditing standards and a complex system of credentialing individuals to do different kinds of work. For example, auditors typically differentiate between *internal* and *external* auditing, the latter involving a report to an outside entity. They also distinguish between *pre-auditing,* which involves an internal control over expenditures, and *post-auditing,* a retrospective review of past performance. Finally, in many jurisdictions, auditing goes beyond a focus on financial transactions to include a broad review of program performance. This expanded activity, *performance auditing,* involves a look at the efficiency and effectiveness of an entity.

The Comptroller General of the United States (1994, p. 14) defines *performance auditing* as: "an objective and systematic examination of evidence for the purpose of providing an independent assessment of the performance of a government organization, program, activity, or function in order to provide information to improve public accountability and facilitate decision-making by parties with responsibility to oversee or initiate corrective action." This definition suggests the increasingly close interface between auditing and evaluation. Because the described activity emerged essentially from financial auditing, its practitioners usually use the term performance auditing.

Program evaluation is a little harder to define than auditing, partly because it has a shorter history as an organized activity and partly because it lacks the formal organizational underpinnings that help to define accounting and auditing. The formal discipline of evaluation has developed mainly since World War II as a response to the growing complexity of social programs and the increasing need for information by decision makers. Because the need has arisen in many different contexts at the same time, it has developed eclectically and it has not fully coalesced as a unified profession in the way auditing has.

Evaluation may be defined as "the systematic application of social research procedures in assessing the conceptualization and design, implementation, and utility of social intervention programs" (Rossi and Freeman, 1985, p. 19). Fundamentally, this involves judging the merit or value of an activity based on a formal, agreed-upon set of procedures grounded in the principles of social science. Social science, of course, is a method of acquiring knowledge based on empirical observation and logic. Therefore, evaluation applies empiricism and reasoning to make judgments about the worth of social programs.

But evaluation is not just an exercise. It supplies information to decision makers who have a responsibility for designing, funding, and implementing programs. A basic assumption of evaluation is that wise decision making requires good, reliable information about how well programs are being managed and how effectively they are accomplishing their goals. Of course, decision makers can make choices without formal evaluation—decision making predates formal evaluation. But the information needs of decision makers have grown as the scope of programs has widened and as the financial stakes have risen.

Auditing and evaluation, then, can be considered two distinct cultures. While both are in the business of assessing performance, they do so from significantly different viewpoints. Chelimsky (1985) has described the major differences and similarities between auditing and evaluation, stressing the two approaches' different origins, contrasting purposes, and diverse viewpoints. While auditing and evaluation share some common characteristics, such as their retrospective viewpoints, emphasis on using systematic processes, and user orientation, she notes that the traditional auditing approach is limited to addressing normative questions. It is also stymied when there are no established criteria for drawing conclusions and can offer few insights about what would have happened in the absence of a program.

Evaluation, in contrast, has several distinct advantages, including a greater ability and willingness to supply relevant descriptive information to decision makers and a capacity to address questions about causality. Evaluation can also provide insights even when there may be a lack of consensus about what a program is supposed to accomplish. Unlike auditing, evaluation "focuses on the relationship between the changes that have been observed and the program, rather than the changes that have been observed and the changes that should have been observed" (Chelimsky, 1985, p. 490).

Finally, evaluation has a broader application and may be ultimately more useful to decision makers than auditing, because it can make assessments about what might happen if a program were implemented differently or if it were absent altogether. This kind of contingent analysis offers decision makers a valuable tool in deliberating about program design and funding.

Davis (1990) has also compared auditing and evaluation, but he stresses some of the auditors' advantages over evaluators. For example, he suggests that managers and policy makers are more likely to use narrow-scope audits that focus on management and accountability than evaluations that address broad policy issues. That is partly because management issues are likely to be easier to understand, are capable of being addressed within a bureaucratic decision-making structure, and are accompanied by far less controversy than analyses of policy. He also notes the gains in credibility that may accrue to auditors, who are organizationally and politically independent from the programs under review and who have long emphasized strict procedures for assuring quality control.

Auditing and evaluating, then, provide two different approaches to assessing organizational performance. Auditors and evaluators operate in many settings—public, private, and nonprofit—in which they do not much interact, but in the state legislative environment they not only work together, they have blended their methods and forged a new way of assessing public organizational performance.

Auditing and Evaluation in the States

It is difficult to describe the work of auditors and evaluators in the fifty states because no two states do things in exactly the same way. Brandeis described the states as "laboratories of democracy," and others have celebrated the capacity of states within a federal system to innovate and experiment. Over the past twenty-five years, the fifty state legislatures have innovated and experimented with a variety of functional and organizational arrangements, many of which are relevant to this discussion.

Before the 1970s, most observers considered state legislatures rather weak and unimportant players on the American political scene. John Gardner observed that "Few institutions in our national life have been as consistently ignored and neglected" as our state legislatures, which, as a result, suffered "grave shortcomings" (Citizens Conference on State Legislatures, 1971, p. viii). Three decades ago, most state legislatures met only a few weeks out of the year, and they had little real organizational capacity. States were less important than the federal government and, within most state governments, legislatures were less important than governors.

But that began to change in the late 1960s. More and more legislatures became full-time institutions, adding staff and becoming professionalized. Legislatures began to streamline their internal operations and develop a greater capacity to perform their constitutional and political functions. The impetus for these changes was complex, but ironically it was partly due to federal government actions, like the creation of Medicaid and block grants, that made states more important partners in the federal system.

In 1969, the New York State Legislature created the Legislative Commission on Expenditure Review, the first state legislative research unit dedicated to overseeing the expenditure of public funds. Other states soon followed suit. The Minnesota Legislature transformed the state's internal pre-audit function (which before 1973 reported to the governor) into an external post-audit function reporting to the legislature, enabling it to conduct more independent, arms-length audits of the executive and judicial branches. Minnesota, like other states, also created a program evaluation unit that could investigate a wide range of issues of interest to the Legislature. By 1980, more than forty states had established some kind of legislative oversight function, employing a total of more than six hundred staff members (Botner, 1986; Brown, 1984; Brown, 1988; Funkhouser, 1984; Green, 1984; Jones, 1987; Wheat, 1991).

Today, according to the National Legislative Program Evaluation Society (NLPES), there are sixty-one state auditing and evaluation units, at least one in each of the fifty state legislatures. Collectively, they employ almost eleven hundred staff members, trained in fields such as accounting, business, economics, political science, sociology, statistics, law, and journalism.

Each unit is nonpartisan and organizationally independent from the entities it audits and evaluates. Most units report to a bipartisan committee of the legislature, sometimes a standing committee, which typically selects topics for evaluation and receives the completed reports. In other respects, the offices differ from one another, largely because of local circumstances and the preferences of decision makers.

One factor differentiating auditing and evaluation units within state legislatures is their organizational location within the legislature. There are three main patterns; a unit may be affiliated with a financial audit office, attached to a budget committee, or established as a free-standing entity.

Of the sixty-one individual state auditing and evaluation units in 1995, 41 percent were attached to financial audit offices, 16 percent were attached to a legislative budget or finance committee, and 43 percent were free-standing units. As might be expected, the organizational location has some effect on the type of work performed, the way each office has employed the services of traditional auditors and evaluators, and the way staff members have adapted their training to the job at hand.

Staffing is a second differentiating factor. In some states, staff members were trained as financial auditors and retrained to do performance auditing. In other states, staff were trained in the social sciences or public affairs. This single factor, for obvious reasons, determines the kind of approach taken in conducting work. But even in those places where traditional auditors predominate, increasingly there is a mix of backgrounds represented on the staff roster. The average office (which has between twelve and fifteen staff members) boasts of staff trained in a variety of fields, from accounting to sociology, mostly at the graduate level.

One telling factor that differentiates among state auditing and evaluation units is whether or not the unit accepts the National State Auditors Association (NSAA) peer review process. The NSAA, which offers the only widely accepted peer review process, establishes whether an office performs its work consistent with the standards of the Comptroller General's *Government Auditing Standards*—the "yellow book," a basic guide used by government financial auditors as well as performance auditors (1994). Several units (including those in Mississippi, Virginia, Minnesota, and Wisconsin) accept the general principles contained in the yellow book, but consider the NSAA peer review inappropriate due to its emphasis on traditional audit process standards. Many other auditing and evaluation units embrace the NSAA peer review.

Despite these differences, state auditing and evaluation units share many characteristics and, as we shall see, have come to adopt a more or less common perspective. While the titles of the offices vary, each unit considers itself part of a national network of state legislative program evaluation (or performance audit) research offices.

Narrowing the Gap Between Auditing and Evaluation

Within the cauldron of state experimentation, change continues to take place. As state legislatures have gained more experience with their auditing and evaluation units, they have begun to learn more about what services auditors and evaluators can and cannot deliver. And auditors and evaluators, for their part, have learned to adapt their work to meet the requirements of their clients.

Although it is still important to distinguish between the auditing approach and the evaluation approach to the assessment of government performance, there are signs that the two approaches may have come closer to each other. No state legislative auditing and evaluation unit follows either a pure auditing approach or a pure evaluation approach. Instead, a kind of amalgamated approach has emerged that draws upon the characteristics of both auditing and evaluation.

Some indicators suggest that the traditional auditing approach is becoming liberalized throughout the profession. One sign of this may be found in the most recent revisions to the yellow book. The latest text acknowledges the validity of nonstandard audits and drops certain previously required audit steps unless they are "significant to audit objectives" (Comptroller General, 1994, pp. 72, 77).

Similarly, the Association of Governmental Accountants' Task Force on Performance Auditing has embraced the notion that "the term 'performance audit' can be applied to a wide range of work," including research performed by social science-trained evaluators ("AGA Task Force," 1993, p. 12). There is a new openness among many traditionally trained auditors to developing new performance auditing techniques that go beyond the narrow-scope auditing of the past. There is also a recognition among more auditors of the limitations, particularly for legislative clients, of standardized audits that focus on an entity's internal controls and management.

At the state level, as mentioned earlier, there are signs that staff hiring patterns in traditional auditing organizations are evolving. One recent survey (Bunderson, 1995, p. 2) showed that about one-third of staff in state legislative auditing and evaluation units have bachelor's degrees in accounting, another one-third have degrees in social sciences, and the remainder have degrees in other fields. But there is an increasing tendency for offices that have taken a traditional auditing approach, such as the Texas State Auditor's Office and the Nevada State Auditor's Office, to hire new staff who have training in the social sciences and public affairs.

There is also a trend toward training existing state audit and evaluation staff in the principles of policy analysis, survey research, and other tools of the social researcher. There is a noticeable increase in in-service training for persons with an accounting background who are seeking additional expertise in these areas. Today, 25 percent of state legislative auditing and evaluation units employ full-time methodologists who provide training for other staff and assist with project research design (Bunderson, 1995, p. 2).

But perhaps the strongest evidence for the liberalization of traditional auditing at the state level is found in the work products of state legislative auditing and evaluation units. Many units have developed a capacity to analyze complex issues from a variety of perspectives. Virginia's Joint Legislative Audit and Review Commission (JLARC) (1990), for example, studied staffing standards that could be used as the basis for distributing state funding to sheriff's offices. The project applied statistical techniques commonly used by social scientists but rarely by traditional auditors. Correlation analysis helped identify workload indicators that were related to staffing levels for each service category. Regression analysis helped determine how much variation in staffing could be explained by the workload indicators identified through the correlation analysis. Based on the results, JLARC staff selected the set of workload measures that best explained variations in staffing, using them in several regression models and formulas to identify an appropriate staffing level for each office receiving state funding.

The Wisconsin Legislative Audit Bureau (1994) has undertaken a multi-year evaluation of that state's Learnfare program, which aims to keep thirteento nineteen-year-old recipients of Aid to Families with Dependent Children (AFDC) in high school. The program reduces AFDC payments to a family if the family's school attendance drops. The Audit Bureau's evaluation uses a classic randomized experimental control-group research design, dividing 3,205 teenagers into a variety of subgroups, enabling the researchers to tell what might have happened in the absence of the program. Preliminary results indicate that the program has a modest impact that varies by population subgroup.

Do these trends mean that the traditional auditing approach is being replaced by the evaluation approach in the states? In some ways, they do. The auditing approach has simply proved too limited in its ability to respond to the needs of state legislatures.

But the approach of evaluators, at least the use by evaluators of the standard approach and protocols of social science research, has also sometimes proven to be ill-suited for the state legislative setting. Some work of evaluators has been too concerned with methodological perfection and insensitive to the rhythms of the legislative client and the language of policy making. Brandl (1980, p. 41) observes that this is not a question of legislators' parochialism, but rather a mismatch between the logic used by evaluators and that used by politicians. "Legislators know that evaluations do not yield truth. They sense that there is some arbitrariness to all scientific work, including evaluation [whose] logical scaffolding rests on assumptions that cannot be verified; evaluations mix dispassionate analysis with political judgments that politicians can make on their own."

Some of the criticisms of evaluators are aimed at those who work outside the legislative setting and whose work was responsive to clients other than the legislature. But a similar response has greeted in-house evaluators who have sometimes been called academic, esoteric, or simply irrelevant. In Minnesota, legislative program evaluation, now an accepted fixture, almost succumbed in its cradle, some say, because of an approach that was too aloof and nonresponsive to its legislative clients.

Instead of adopting either the traditional auditing approach or the social science–based evaluation approach in its pure form, many state legislative auditing and evaluation units have developed a middle course. This middle course, or what may be called the *blended approach,* has the following characteristics:

• *It places a high value on independence—from its client as well as from the entity under examination.* Legislative auditors and evaluators have learned that their credibility rests on independence as well as technical prowess. The sometimes adversarial relationships that develop between legislative auditors and evaluators on one hand and those whose programs are under review on the other would be anathema to many evaluators working in other settings, but they are normal for most auditors. While relations with the legislative client are never adversarial, they are generally distant and always nonpartisan.

• *It stresses the need for painstaking research documentation and extensive internal review procedures.* These steps are generally not the result of client demand; they derive from the need for credibility. Those who are under review more often accept the fairness of an audit or evaluation if they are reassured that it is conducted according to strict professional standards and controls. Most state legislative auditing and evaluation units have developed elaborate policies for organizing and keeping project *working papers*—documents that can be inspected by those who want to know how findings and conclusions were arrived at. Internal review policies usually ensure that the evidence and analyses of audit and evaluation reports are checked extensively before they are published.

• *It uses multiple methodologies, including shortcuts and quick analysis techniques that provide information quickly to clients.* State legislative auditing and evaluation units only rarely use experimental designs, because they are costly, not-timely, and ill-suited for addressing typical research assignments. But there is a willingness and a capacity to use many other common research techniques, including survey research, focus groups, case studies, multiple regression using existing data, systematic interviews, and other tools of social science research.

• *It addresses issues of wide scope, often providing users with contextual information and broad analyses of whole programs, rather than narrow functional issues.* State legislative auditors and evaluators do not always look at whole programs, but they are increasingly willing to follow a twisting trail through a complex bureaucratic and policy maze to examine issues of interest to their clients.

• *It is suitable for answering almost any kind of question—normative and descriptive questions as well as those that focus on causality.* Legislators typically want answers to questions like What is going on in government programs and agencies? How did the money that we appropriated get spent? Was the program implemented as we directed? Is the program being managed well? Is the program reaching its goals? What can be done to improve the program? These questions touch on matters of accountability and good management as well as program design and policy alternatives.

The first two of these characteristics derive from the auditing approach, the next two derive from the evaluation approach, and the last draws upon both approaches. As noted earlier, there are still important differences among state legislative auditing and evaluation units, and it would be misleading to imply that the blended approach describes the perspective of all. But there is a perceptible trend toward a common approach that relies on elements from both the auditing and the evaluation traditions.

Why a New Approach Is Emerging

From the vantage point of the state legislatures, the reasons for this evolutionary development are plain. They are rooted in the institution of the legislature itself and flow naturally from the diverse roles that legislatures play in state governmental systems.

Like any client who looks for professional assistance in solving a problem, legislators are less concerned with the methods of professionals than with the products they can deliver. As the AGA Task Force (1993, p. 13) pointed out,

"Policy makers [want] reliable facts and sound, independent professional judgment, and they care little about . . . terminology. They use terms like performance auditing and program evaluation interchangeably. Their greatest concern is that they get answers to their most pressing questions about the performance of government programs and agencies."

State legislative auditors and evaluators have begun to adopt a blended approach to their work, stressing elements of both auditing and evaluation, because state legislatures need and want the products that derive from both auditing and evaluation. Although state legislatures existed for almost two centuries without much help from professional auditors or evaluators, today those professionals play an important role in assisting state legislatures with their most vital functions—making policy, allocating public money, and overseeing the implementation of public programs. In each of these areas, state auditors and evaluators have found ways to provide information and analyses that, over the past twenty-five years, legislatures have come to depend upon.

Because of local preference or organizational location, some state units have stressed their ability to help the legislature with one of these fundamental roles more than another. But perhaps the most successful state auditing and evaluation units are those that have emphasized assisting in all three areas.

Legislative Oversight. Of the three legislative functions, state auditors and evaluators play their most significant role in legislative oversight. Mirroring the structure of the federal government, each state government is organized into three more or less coequal branches that share state powers. Within this general scheme, state legislatures have the power and responsibility to check on the actions of the other two branches of government to ensure that they are behaving properly. This arrangement reflects a fundamental tenet of American political philosophy—that concentrated power eventually leads to tyranny and needs to be checked.

Traditionally, state legislatures have exercised control over the executive mainly by giving and withholding money or by approving and disapproving personnel appointments. But legislators have long been dissatisfied with their ability to oversee the other branches and hold them accountable. They have been at a particular disadvantage in their ability to do fact finding and technical analysis. Public hearings are not particularly well suited for these purposes, mainly because of the difficulty of receiving balanced and objective testimony that can be verified. Also, public hearings are subject to abuse by the legislature itself and, unless conducted with judiciousness and discernment, can lack credibility among the parties involved.

The creation of specialized audit and evaluation staff offices has helped to address this shortcoming in many states. As a result, legislators have an alternative method of gathering information on which to base decisions. Not unlike military commanders, legislators can send reconnaissance units into enemy territory to bring back intelligence from the field. They can dispatch auditors and evaluators to examine agency files, interview program clients, evaluate program performance, examine management's track record, and check the records to see how appropriated money was spent. According to Rosenthal (1983), this has contributed to a major shift in the balance of power between governors and legislators. Legislatures have now become the "first branch of state government," clearly the "dominant partner" in many states (p. 90).

State legislative auditors and evaluators have been able to perform this role for several reasons. They possess a range of technical skills, are afforded adequate time and resources to probe, have privileged access in some areas to data on public programs (often buttressed by the subpoena power), and enjoy a standing with legislative bodies that derives from their nonpartisanship, independence, and track record.

Staff who are trained in the traditional auditing approach are comfortable with legislative oversight assignments because a great deal of oversight involves checking to see if public officials are in compliance with laws, regulations, and legislative intent. The traditional auditing approach, with its emphasis on answering normative questions and verifying compliance with standards, is well suited to help the legislature exercise legislative oversight.

Budget Making. In some places, state legislative auditors and evaluators have also carved out a prominent role as legislative budget analysts. In some states, auditors and evaluators work under direction of legislative fiscal or budget committees, sometimes for just one house of the legislature and other times for both houses. In these cases, auditors and evaluators have a direct role in influencing the state budget. In other states, the relationship between the budget process and auditors and evaluators is more informal.

Budget making is often considered the most important legislative function because it deals with setting public priorities and deciding how much money gets distributed to various public programs. Budget committees of the legislature are considered more powerful than standing policy committees because most programs can only function with tangible resources.

In those states where legislative auditing and evaluation is structurally a part of the legislature's budget or fiscal committees, staff members operate near the heart of the legislative budget process. They assist by determining what happened to past appropriations and analyzing the cost-effectiveness of budget alternatives. The analysis performed in these situations is often somewhat limited, given the way budget committees operate, but the interim period between legislative sessions offers an opportunity for longer-term studies and the application of methodologies other than straight cost-benefit analysis.

In those states where there is no formal tie between the auditing and evaluation unit and the budget committees, the role of auditors and evaluators in budget making is less direct. But in recent years, budget committees nevertheless have tried to get auditors and evaluators to address two kinds of budget-relevant questions: Where can savings be found to help balance the budget or reduce spending, and what is the likely fiscal impact of alternative courses of state action? Interestingly, many legislative auditing and evaluation offices have justified their own future funding based on their track record in identifying cost savings from executive branch agencies.

Policy Making. Finally, state legislative auditors and evaluators have begun to help legislatures perform their policy-making function. Although some legislators do not welcome legislative staff becoming involved in policy questions, mainly because they perceive policy making to be the exclusive domain of elected officials, many see a valid role for evaluators. Increasingly, legislative auditors and evaluators have provided background and contextual information about programs or agencies, identified and highlighted issues, and offered analyses of alternative policy decisions.

But auditors and evaluators seldom make recommendations favoring one policy alternative over another, mainly because they lack the political standing to do so. When such recommendations are made, it is common to make them contingent. In Minnesota, for example, legislative program evaluators studied the impact of various factors on workers' compensation premium rates, concluding that high benefits contributed the most to making Minnesota's rates among the nation's highest. Evaluators recommended that, *if the legislature wanted to lower premiums,* it could do so by reducing certain benefits (Minnesota Office of the Legislative Auditor, 1988).

But there are clearly limits to the application and effectiveness of this policy role. As Brandl (1980, p. 41) has pointed out, legislators know that "all truth cannot be captured by an evaluation and that truth in any event does not always carry necessary implications for policy." While acknowledging the key role of evaluators to confront politicians with "explicit statements of what is going on," Brandl implies that evaluators will wear out their welcome if they do not recognize that policy making is fundamentally a political process rather than a rational one.

Legislative auditors and evaluators also have difficulty in playing a high-profile policy advocacy role because they are internal to a process that is dominated by their bosses. Their main stock in trade—their independence and credibility—enhances their effectiveness in addressing policy questions, but may itself be jeopardized by taking sides in political disputes.

Overall Approach. Today's legislative auditors and evaluators are somewhat like baseball switch hitters, capable of responding to the occasion. When the legislature calls for an oversight study, a budget review, or a policy analysis, the response is skillful, competent, and credible. Even when a study involves a variety of diverse questions—including normative, descriptive, and cause-and-effect questions—and requires the use of a complex, multimethod research design, most state legislative auditing and evaluation units can rise to the occasion.

They have also developed close working relationships with their respective legislative bodies. Individual staff work closely with individual members and committees of the legislature, at least for the duration of a particular study. This personalization of the auditing and evaluation process strengthens the tie between researcher and client, improving the overall level of responsiveness to the client.

Conclusion: Lessons for Others

Emerson argued that there is no false logic in nature. Likewise, there is a certain inescapability in the development of auditing and evaluation within the state legislatures because it has arisen from the nature of the legislative institution itself. Where local conditions vary, so does the complexion of auditing and evaluation.

To be sure, the two cultures of auditing and evaluation still exist. Particularly when comparing approaches across states, one still observes important differences. But they are declining, mostly because of a liberalization of traditional auditing.

The emergence of a blended approach to auditing and evaluation in the states is probably not unique. It is possible that a similar trend is apparent at the federal level, particularly at the General Accounting Office, and perhaps in other jurisdictions at home and abroad.

Auditors and evaluators who work in other kinds of settings may gain from considering the experience of state legislative auditors and evaluators. Key factors in their success include:

- *Professionalism.* Adoption of professional standards and adherence to widely accepted protocols have lent credibility and weight to the work of auditors and evaluators operating on behalf of state legislatures, even though the environment itself is volatile and highly political.
- *Responsiveness.* State legislative auditors and evaluators have adapted their work to match the complex roles played by legislative institutions. They have developed an ability to respond to a wide range of questions and to generate a variety of products.
- *Flexibility.* State legislative auditors and evaluators have been willing to try new approaches. The two groups have learned from each other, freely borrowing techniques and perspectives from one another, and have gradually forged an approach that suits the changing needs of legislatures.

The environment of state legislative auditing and evaluation can be volatile and the stakes can be high. Fundamentally, it is a political environment. But by stressing professionalism, remaining responsive to the needs of the institution within which they work, and remaining flexible and open to alternative ways of operating, legislative auditors and evaluators have thrived. Their work may become more important and visible as the states become more significant partners in the federal system.

References

"AGA Task Force Report on Performance Auditing." *Government Accountants Journal,* 1993, 42 (2), 11–25.

Botner, S. B. "Trends and Developments in State Postauditing." *State and Local Government Review,* Winter 1986, pp. 13–19.

Brandl, J. *Policy Evaluation and the Work of Legislatures.* New Directions for Program Evaluation, no. 5. San Francisco: Jossey-Bass, 1980.

Brown, J. R. "Legislative Program Evaluation: Defining a Legislative Service and a Profession." *Public Administration Review,* 1984, *44* (3), 258–260.

Brown, J. R. "State Evaluation in a Legislative Environment: Adapting Evaluation to Legislative Needs." In C. G. Wye and H. P. Hatry (eds.), *Timely, Low-Cost Evaluation in the Public Sector.* New Directions for Program Evaluation, no. 38. San Francisco: Jossey-Bass, 1988.

Bunderson, J. T. "Study of the States on Selected Legislative Program Evaluation Characteristics." Unpublished paper, Idaho Legislative Services, 1995.

Chelimsky, E. "Comparing and Contrasting Auditing and Evaluation: Some Notes on Their Relationship." *Evaluation Review,* 1985, *9* (4), 483–503.

Citizens Conference on State Legislatures. *The Sometime Governments.* New York: Bantam, 1971.

Comptroller General of the United States. *Government Auditing Standards, 1994 Revision.* Washington, D.C.: U.S. General Accounting Office, 1994.

Davis, D. "Do You Want a Performance Audit or a Program Evaluation?" *Public Administration Review,* Jan./Feb. 1990, pp. 35–41.

Funkhouser, M. "Current Issues in Legislative Program Evaluation." *Public Administration Review,* 1984, *44* (3), 261–264.

Green, A. "The Role of Evaluation in Legislative Decision Making." *Public Administration Review,* 1984, *44* (3), 265–267.

Jones, R. "Keeping an Eye on State Agencies." *State Legislatures,* July 1987, pp. 20–23.

Kuhn, T. S. *The Structure of Scientific Revolutions.* Chicago: University of Chicago Press, 1962.

Minnesota Office of the Legislative Auditor, Program Evaluation Division. *Workers' Compensation Program.* St. Paul: Minnesota Office of the Legislative Auditor, Feb. 1988.

Rosenthal, A. "Legislative Oversight and the Balance of Power in State Government." *State Government,* 1983, *53* (3), 90–98.

Rossi, P. H., and Freeman, H. E. *Evaluation: A Systematic Approach.* Thousand Oaks, Calif.: Sage, 1985.

Snow, C. P. *The Two Cultures and the Scientific Revolution.* New York: Cambridge University Press, 1959.

Virginia Joint Legislative Audit and Review Commission. *Technical Review: Staffing Standards for the Funding of Sheriffs.* Richmond: Virginia Joint Legislative Audit and Review Commission, Feb. 1990.

Wheat, E. M. "The Activist Auditor: A New Player in State and Local Politics." *Public Administration Review,* 1991, *51* (5), 385–393.

Wisconsin Legislative Audit Bureau. *An Evaluation of Wisconsin's Learnfare Program: Summary of an Interim Report on First-Semester Effects.* Madison: Wisconsin Legislative Audit Bureau, 1994.

ROGER A. BROOKS is deputy legislative auditor for program evaluation, Minnesota Office of the Legislative Auditor.

A comparison is made of the ways in which evaluators and performance auditors address a series of issues common to both. Based mainly on British and Finnish practice, it is suggested that the most important differences may lie less in the tools and methods used than in the framework of institutional relationships within which the activities are carried out.

Performance Audit and Evaluation: Similar Tools, Different Relationships?

Christopher Pollitt, Hilkka Summa

Since at least the late 1970s, performance audit (or *value-for-money audit* as it is sometimes termed) has taken state audit institutions far beyond their traditional concerns with financial probity and regularity. At different speeds in different countries, state audit institutions (SAIs) developed new activities focused on questions of program efficiency and effectiveness. More recently, they have also moved into questions of public service quality.

There can be little doubt that these developments have brought auditing closer to evaluation. At the same time, the dominant modes of evaluation have also been shifting. The ambitious experimental approaches that were attempted in the United States during the late 1960s and early 1970s have long since given way to a more diverse set of approaches to evaluation, with rather pragmatic evaluations in the service of senior management becoming perhaps the most common single type during the 1980s and 1990s. Not surprisingly, these various convergences have raised a number of questions about the border territory between evaluation and performance audit. These have included:

- How far can (and should) performance auditors borrow tools, techniques, and methods from evaluation.
- How far do SAIs need to recruit and train their auditors differently now that they are expected to conduct performance audits as well as regulatory audits.
- What is the nature of the remaining differences (if any) between audit and evaluation.

An interesting literature has begun to grow up around these questions (for example, Chelimsky, 1985; Dekker and Leeuw, 1989; Rist, 1989). The

NEW DIRECTIONS FOR EVALUATION, no. 71, Fall 1996 © Jossey-Bass Publishers key features of this debate will be discussed later in this chapter, as it is one of our objectives to develop the discussion about similarities and differences between the two sets of activities. However, what has been noticeable by its absence from the literature thus far is any systematic empirical comparison between matched samples of audits and evaluations. Instead, most contributors have offered broad conceptual analyses illustrated by particular examples. The present chapter also falls within this genre, although its authors are currently engaged in a more systematic, empirically based project that they hope will result in future publications of a more thoroughly grounded character.

The main objective of the chapter is to seek a better interpretive understanding of the activity of performance audit. We approach this by examining the similarities and differences between performance audit and evaluation. However, ours is not an evenhanded treatment of the two activities—the main focus is on performance audit and the characteristics (and variations) of evaluation are much more lightly sketched.

The main evidential base for the chapter is the general literature on audit and evaluation, especially that referring to the activities of SAIs in Europe. More specifically, we draw on casework research and a modest number of interviews with key audit staff. Our main focus has been on the U.K. National Audit Office (NAO), the U.K. Audit Commission, and the Finnish State Audit Office (SAO).

Audit and Evaluation: Some Preliminary Remarks

At their most basic, both audit and evaluation involve one set of people (the auditors or evaluators) going out to scrutinize and assess the activities of another set of people (the auditees or evaluees). In both cases, the upshot of the assessment is usually a report of some kind. Our approach is to build on these basic similarities by identifying a series of steps or stages through which both performance auditors and evaluators are obliged to go. For each of these stages, we describe what we consider to be the problems facing performance audit and then examine the key similarities and differences as compared with evaluation. In our concluding reflections, we attempt to come to an overall view of these and to identify where the most significant differences appear to lie.

Many of the major points of contrast between audit and evaluation were established in a definitive article by Chelimsky (1985). In this chapter, we draw on that source but also go beyond it. It is important to bear in mind that Chelimsky was, in the main, contrasting evaluation with traditional (financial or regularity) audit whereas we shall focus almost exclusively on a newer type of activity—performance audit. Chelimsky's model remains relevant, however, because much of the culture and authority of state audit institutions (and the practices that flow from these) are still deeply influenced by their history as promoters of regularity and probity in the use of public finance.

It is important to note that our comparison is between the activities of SAIs and *external* evaluations. This chapter does not deal with internal evaluations or the self-evaluating organization. In this context, it is worth bearing in mind that, in the field of external evaluations of public programs, the tendency of the last decade or more has been for a high proportion of such evaluations to be commissioned by state executive bodies of one kind or another (ministries, health authorities, local governments, and so on) and for many of these evaluations to have adopted a managerialist approach (for the U.K. experience, see Pollitt, 1993).

Chelimsky first identifies significant differences in the origins of audit and evaluation. The former is older, and grew out of the practical concerns of early modern bookkeeping. Evaluation, as a labeled and self-conscious set of activities, appeared in the 1960s, mainly in the United States. It was one of the many offshoots of the huge post-war growth in the social sciences in American universities, and to this day retains an unauditlike concern with theory and explanation rather than with the verification of authoritative documents. Certainly—in the bold days of its youth—evaluation aspired to be a science, and some of its practitioners still hanker after that status.

Audit developed under the assumptions that agreed and fixed criteria were to be applied to a set of accounts (verification), following which the results of that comparison would be reported to a clearly identified client. The world of evaluation was, from the outset, less certain. The selection of criteria, instead of being professionally given, was on most occasions very much part of the problem to be solved. And instead of a singular client, a variety of audiences frequently demanded consideration—the body or bodies paying for the evaluation, to be sure, but also professionals, politicians, governments, and even the wider public.

As different schools of evaluation developed, some began to lay great stress on forming cooperative, interactive relationships with those who were being evaluated (evaluees). One aim here was to maximize the chances that the evaluation's recommendations would prove acceptable and implementable. Increasingly, from the mid-1970s, this emphasis on the need to learn from and convince the subjects of the evaluation replaced the earlier image of the evaluator as a dispassionate scientist of society. The evaluator became more of a down-to-earth engineer, for whom it was important to talk to those who operated the machines (programs, projects) and those who used the goods and services that were thereby produced. This model of evaluation as a form of interactive learning reached a peak in the work of Guba and Lincoln (1989), with their notion of "fourth generation evaluation." Such an approach contrasts starkly with the assumptions (traditional in orthodox financial audit) of the puritanically independent auditor who largely confines his or her attention to the black print in the key authoritative documents.

If evaluation was a less certain activity than audit, there was compensation in that it seemed an intellectually more exciting one. Auditors checked to see whether what had been done conformed to standards—a What question. Evaluators endeavored to understand what would produce certain desired (and undesired) effects—a Why question. Although auditors might claim to increase the transparency and therefore accountability of public bodies, evaluators could hold out the vision of an *experimenting society* (see Chapter 4 of Shadish, Cook, and Leviton, 1991). Also, evaluators frequently claim that one of their major contributions is to reformulate issues and encourage stakeholders to see problems in different ways. The extent to which specific recommendations are implemented is an inadequate measure of the overall impact of an evaluation (Greenberg and Mandell, 1991).

The business of explaining *why* some particular impact or effect has occurred was identified by Rist (1989) as one of the most fundamental differences between audit and evaluation. Rist argued that audit, by working to a criterion-referenced design, did not permit auditors to rule out competing explanations for why a program or policy achieved (or failed to achieve) its intended results. Thus the analysis of the effectiveness of a program was a task Rist assigned to evaluation rather than audit. However, not everyone holds this view. A number of commentators who have supported the development of performance audit argue that the causes of effectiveness or ineffectiveness can be directly addressed by audit teams (see, for example, Dekker and Leeuw, 1989).

In one important respect, however, SAIs retained a major advantage over their new evaluator cousins. They possessed statutory clout of a kind that specialist evaluation organizations rarely if ever achieved. The evaluation literature of the 1970s and 1980s is full of musings about why the recommendations of evaluators so often lie neglected and ignored by public authorities. However, when SAIs undertake investigations, matters are somewhat different. Auditors usually wield rights of access to defined categories of executive papers. Accounting officers can be summoned to appear and give evidence. Ministries of finance, treasuries, and other audited departments and agencies are often (not always—this is an interesting point of difference among SAIs) obliged to publish reasoned responses to auditors' reports. Special committees of legislatures make it their business to pursue the executive authorities and satisfy themselves that the latter are taking the audit recommendations seriously. Of course, governments can and frequently do reject the recommendations of SAIs, but usually not without at least a show of polite consideration.

What is interesting about the recent expansion of performance audit (as distinct from traditional financial or compliance audit) is that SAIs appear to retain this distinctive (sometimes coercive) authority although they are now moving out into much less certain territories and using a wider range of analytical tools. However, the basis for this authority is beginning to be questioned (for example, see Power, 1994).

A final preliminary observation concerns the dangers of confusing the actual with the ideal. Both evaluation and performance audit are extremely sophisticated activities that, at their best, may yield compelling and even counterintuitive insights into the workings of government programs and policies. Much of the existing literature concerns, in effect, the *potential* of these activities, that is, what they may achieve when carried out by the most skillful practitioners under ideal circumstances. In practice, of course, both performance audits and evaluations frequently fall well short of their theoretical potential. Thus, for example, it would be quite wrong to suppose that, in practice, most evaluations are able to develop convincing cause-and-effect analyses of the final impacts of public programs and the reasons for these impacts. Indeed, quite a few experienced evaluators would probably say that in their craft such achievements are the exception rather than the rule. In practice, the kinds of analyses carried out by evaluators and performance auditors may overlap rather more than would be suggested by a pure analysis of the models underlying these two activities.

Choosing What to Investigate

This is the first step. SAIs usually devise *programs* of activity. They do not choose topics at random. Top management attempt to balance several factors. One of these will be the volume of public resources involved in an activity—its fiscal salience. SAIs will normally give some priority to high-cost programs. In the United Kingdom, schools are usually the biggest expenditure item in local authority budgets and soon became a focus for a special study by the newly created Audit Commission (Henkel, 1991). In Finland, economic importance is one of the four criteria given to guide topic choice for SAO auditors (State Audit Office, 1995a). SAIs may be especially drawn toward programs where budgets appear to have fallen more slowly than demand for the service in question or where budgets have risen without there being a corresponding and clearly identifiable increase in quality or productivity.

A second common criterion for choosing the territory is the risk to public funds. For example, new high-technology investments are likelier to present high risks than routine licensing operations. This is one reason why the procurement of advanced military equipment and facilities is a frequent focus for SAIs (for example, National Audit Office, 1994b, 1994d). High-tech civil R&D may also come under scrutiny (National Audit Office, 1994a).

The political salience of an activity is a third criterion, though one that SAIs are understandably sometimes uneasy about discussing (or may even deny). However, ultimately they work for political clients—whether in the legislature or the executive. If these politicians are to be satisfied, at least a proportion of audits must explore territory of current political interest. For example, a NAO study of the Trident works program, though not hitherto particularly salient in the NAO's strategic plan, was promoted straight to the preliminary study stage when the works program began to receive hostile comment in the Scottish press and from Scottish Members of Parliament (MPs) (National Audit Office, 1994b).

However, the opportunity for *direct* political input to the choice of topic varies considerably according to the particular institutional position of the SAI in question—for example, direct input is unlikely in the case of the SAO but explicitly provided for (through the Public Accounts Committee) in the case of the NAO. Even with the SAO, however, some projects may be chosen partly on the basis of requests from the parliamentary state auditor.

Fourth, SAIs need to pay attention to what has been done before. There is an obvious argument for making "a systematic coverage of the audit field over a period of years" (Comptroller and Auditor General, 1993, para 4). Thus, for example, the NAO study *Creating and Safeguarding Jobs in Wales* (National Audit Office, 1991) emerged from a strategic planning process that envisaged a series of NAO investigations of government bodies in Wales (Roberts and Pollitt, 1994, p. 532).

Finally, there is likelihood that investigation of a particular topic will yield useful new knowledge that could contribute to improvements or be applied to other areas of state activity. The SAO's criteria include that of the potential fruitfulness of a topic (State Audit Office, 1995a).

There are thus a number of fairly common and defensible criteria by which SAIs choose topics for investigation. Nevertheless, it would be a considerable exaggeration to claim that such choices were usually scientific or even predictably formulaic. The U.K., Canadian, and Australian cases studied by Sloan (1995) demonstrate that the preferences of individuals in SAIs are frequently influential. Our own work with the NAO and the SAO reinforce this impression. This brings us to the question of SAIs' room for maneuvering.

In finding promising topics, auditors experience both advantages and disadvantages compared with evaluators. Their biggest advantage is that, in principle at least, SAIs can sit back and decide what to investigate. In the NAO's case, for example, the Comptroller and Auditor General can choose what to investigate; the organization is not instructed to look at this but not at that. Similarly, the SAO enjoys statutory autonomy in its choice of topics.

SAIs can and do develop programs of audits more or less systematically covering particular sectors or topics over a period of years. Very few evaluators enjoy this kind of freedom. Evaluations are usually more ad hoc affairs. An evaluation team is hired to analyze a topic or problem or program that has been chosen by someone else (the body commissioning the evaluation).

However, evaluators also possess some partially countervailing advantages. Audit tends to be focused on particular procedures, programs, or institutions. The founding documents of SAIs usually refer to their core business as assuring regularity, economy, efficiency, and (sometimes) effectiveness in public spending programs. Evaluators sometimes enjoy greater freedom to define the objects of their investigations as a particular problem or issue rather than a program. Theoretically and methodologically there is obviously much to be said for this broader approach—for investigations of homelessness (the issue) rather than the public housing program of department X or for investigations of criminal behavior (the issue) rather than an audit of the prison program or the courts or the police (the programs and institutions). Evaluators may also have rather more freedom to propose and carry out comparative analyses—of crime or homelessness (or whatever) in different cities or regions or countries. SAIs may find this more difficult because it may involve them in complicated and sensitive approach and clearance procedures with a number of different public bodies. It can be easier to choose just one program run by one agency. At a more basic level, SAIs will commonly be focused on particular lines of expenditure—on specified financial flows rather than on broader conceptual issues. State funding rather than causation is their defining criterion for topic definition.

Unfortunately, in the real world, evaluators get to exercise their greater theoretical freedom only rarely (Hellstern, 1991, p. 302). More commonly, the commissioning body will define the object for evaluation as a given project or program, constraining the evaluator in much the same way as the auditor is usually constrained. Indeed, there is a sense in which evaluations come into being only when they are demanded whereas audits are supplied, insofar as SAIs already exist to carry them out.

Resourcing the Investigation

Like any other organizational activity, audits take time and cost money. SAIs have to cost their activities and demonstrate that they themselves embody the principle of value for money (VFM). The U.K. National Audit Office (NAO) has a global annual savings target and claims to save £7 for every £1 it spends (National Audit Office, 1994c, p. 2). The average cost of an NAO VFM audit is currently around £180,000. Auditors are judged by their own top managers partly by their ability to complete audits on time and within budget, while pointing to substantial savings or efficiency gains. Likewise the SAO has a systematic annual planning procedure. The auditor general establishes *results agreements* with heads of units. The number of planned work days is spelled out for each investigation and the costs and results achieved are compared to targets and annually reported (State Audit Office, 1995a, 1995b).

Yet it would be rash to assume that the full costs of audits were always carefully estimated and comfortably exceeded by the benefits. Apart from the usual questions about how fairly overheads have been allocated, there are larger issues about the financial and opportunity costs that auditors in effect impose on their audited bodies. Once the audited body knows that the auditors are coming, it is likely to spend a good deal of time and effort tidying up at home. Such auditee compliance costs do not appear in the SAIs' accounts. In the private sector, by contrast, audit compliance costs have become the focus of considerable measurement effort and debate.

The situation of evaluators is typically somewhat different. At the outset they need to sell their product to the commissioning body, and pricing the evaluation is very much part of that process (especially where, as is increasingly the case in the United Kingdom, evaluations are the subject of competitive tendering procedures). Often the commissioner will already have a maximum figure in mind, so the package of people and methods to be employed in the evaluation will have to be shaped to fit that figure. Even though SAIs are usually working with fixed global budgets, they would seem to possess a greater degree of freedom than most evaluators in respect of determining the resourcing of each individual investigation. They are in a portfolio situation where in principle they could choose to make project A much bigger by scrapping or downsizing projects B and C. Occasionally evaluation units may be able to do something similar, for example by offering a project at cost or as a loss leader to an important new client. However, neither in the United Kingdom nor in most other European countries are there enough large and well-established evaluation units to be able thus to maneuver within a broad portfolio. This may be a significant difference between Europe and the United States. The latter has a longer, deeper history of evaluation and supports a number of prestigious evaluatory institutions that may sometimes be able to play portfolio, at least to some extent.

Assembling an Investigatory Team

Performance or VFM audits call for more than conventional accountancy skills. Statisticians, economists, management experts, and a host of other specialists (including evaluators) may be necessary if a particular topic is to be properly understood, and if the auditors are going to protect themselves from later accusations that they were ignorant and misunderstood what they saw or found. When the U.K. Audit Commission decided to carry out a study of National Health Service (NHS) pathology laboratories, it consulted closely with the Royal College of Pathologists and the Association of Medical Laboratory Officers. Specialists with a background in management techniques and organizational development plus experience of working in the NHS were hired and given special training (Audit Commission, 1993; Longdon, 1995).

Similarly, the NAO frequently employs expert consultants for its studies, and there have been occasions when they have made influential suggestions concerning the design and contents of a particular investigation. The co-option of experts clearly offers two-way advantages in that it provides safeguards to the SAIs and also assures powerful professions or other groups that their voice will be heard.

In Finland, however, the SAO usually does not hire consultants (though the possibility of doing so is currently contemplated and some budgetary provision for this has been made). Instead, the SAO has put effort into in-house training for performance auditors. It could be argued that this strategy puts the SAO at greater risk than other SAIs of having reports challenged on grounds of lack of expertise.

It is an interesting question whether brought-in experts remain on tap to the auditors or may even become on top as far as influencing the content of the final report is concerned. During the Audit Commission study *Towards Better Management of Secondary Education,* there was evidently an important debate between members of the team with an audit background and those educationalists who had been brought in from Local Education Authorities (Audit Commission, 1986). The first draft of the full report was written by an academic consultant. However, the Controller of the Audit Commission himself then intervened and insisted on important changes (Henkel, 1991, pp. 36–41).

Of course, evaluators also face the need to assemble teams with appropriate skills to tackle specialist topics. However, academic evaluators tend to be more closely linked to the social science community, and are therefore bearers of assumptions about academic expertise and participants in (or eavesdroppers upon) ongoing debates concerning scientific methodologies. Auditors, by contrast, constitute a distinct occupational group possessing specific professional qualifications and observing national or international standards. Such standards carry an official status that is foreign to most of the contemporary, post-positivist world of the social sciences.

Contacting the Subjects of the Investigation

External auditors are usually regarded with a mixture of curiosity, anxiety, and downright fear by the staff of the institutions they have chosen for report. In practice, the audited body is usually contacted early on. However, early negotiations are conditioned by both parties' awareness that an SAI usually has the *right* to insist on access. The SAO provides a fairly pure example of such rights in that the State Audit Act requires auditees, upon request, to "display to the competent auditor or deliver to the Audit Office those books, account statements and other documents that are necessary for the purposes of auditing or controlling, and without delay provide the Office or the auditor with the information or explanations requested."

Early contacts are often significant for a variety of reasons. Auditees may take the opportunity to attempt to influence the precise track of the audit and the methods to be used. For example, in the NAO's case, departments and agencies are adept at arguing that their particular operation is in important respects unique, and that any comparative data that auditors might be thinking of compiling would be unreliable or actively misleading. This may be one of the reasons why certain reports either omitted rather obvious opportunities for overseas comparisons or attempted them only within very limited compass. For example, see National Audit Office (1993a) on motorway widening projects, and (1994a) on renewable energy research and development.

In our interviews, SAO officials argued that direct resistance from auditees was not part of their experience. However, they very much recognized the importance for an auditor of establishing at an early stage a good dialogue with the natives. Indeed, the latter might play a role in the investigation itself: for example, a performance audit of state subsidies to technology and product development included a sample of over eight hundred projects in which staff of the audited body did much of the data collection and processing (State Audit Office, 1991).

One promising tactic for SAIs is to recruit senior staff from the area to be audited onto the investigative teams. Many examples present themselves. One striking instance occurred with the Audit Commission's investigation of medical records (Audit Commission, 1995). Here a group of doctors, nurses, health care managers, and other locals were recruited to draft a set of principles of good practice that subsequently became a centerpiece of the final report. The co-option of such experts serves several purposes. It helps the auditors to know where to look and who to contact during the expedition. It deprives the auditees of any chance of presenting a united front of resistance, since some of their own are already working for the auditors. It reduces the probability that the auditors will end up saying anything that may betray their lack of thorough acquaintance with the topic under investigation. In short, it provides both legitimacy and expertise. It is interesting, therefore, that while the Audit Commission and the NAO regularly take advantage of these possibilities the SAO has so far seemed much more reluctant to dilute the purity of action of individual auditors.

It is clear that many of the issues that have been referred to in this section are also faced by evaluators. It is prudent or, indeed, essential for evaluators to negotiate access (but usually without the big stick of statutory rights of access in their back pockets). Evaluation designs are, like audits, frequently modified as a result of early discussions with those who are to be evaluated. Sensible evaluators take on board experts from the territory they are about to explore—all these features are common.

What may be different, however, is the view taken of the temporal dimension of the evaluator-evaluee relationship. Evaluators are frequently performing one particular evaluation. This may be their first—and may well be their last—contact with the particular program or agency being evaluated. SAIs, by contrast, more usually enjoy a continuing relationship with major public departments and agencies within their audit field. They have probably done audits in department X before. They may already be planning to undertake further audits there in their future program. They may therefore be at least marginally more concerned to preserve good relations—not to queer the pitch for audits yet to come. Of course, if an evaluation organization has a continuing relationship with a major customer (like, say, the RAND Corporation and the U.S. Department of Defense), then such considerations apply to them too. In Europe, however, many evaluations will not fall into this SAI-like category, and the calculation is therefore likely to be more ad hoc.

These temporal differences, combined with the different status external evaluators are often seen as having (for example, "just some academics"), may either help or hinder evaluators. Auditees may be more cautious in speaking to the representative of a powerful SAI, and feel less inhibited with a one-off visiting academic, especially if the latter is an expert in the particular topic. Alternatively if the evaluation is not seen as likely to carry much clout the visiting academics may be dismissed after minimal provision of information.

Planning and Designing Studies

Performance audits are by definition journeys into the unknown or partly known. SAIs frequently build in a preliminary investigation phase before committing themselves to a full study. After this, the task may appear simpler than it did before. More commonly, perhaps, unforeseen difficulties may emerge.

Occasionally performance audits are actually abandoned or radically scaled down at this stage. This is said to be rare in the NAO but appears less so at the SAO. In 1993, the SAO dropped five investigations on the basis of preliminary studies (representing about 16 percent of the performance audits they undertook that year). The decision to abort is typically made by the audit councillor; SAO staff indicate that a low probability of making important or fruitful findings is the most common reason.

Two types of topic that tend to pose particular difficulties are those categorized as *policy* or *professional* (Henkel, 1991, pp. 34–70). An example of a political no-go area can be found in the NAO report on the Pergau Dam project in Malaysia. This dam was financed by £234 million of U.K. overseas aid funds despite the fact that prior internal evaluations of the project appeared to indicate that it was not a good investment. The NAO report told the story of these internal analyses and concluded that the "chosen method of implementation would cost the U.K. £56M more than it might otherwise have done" (National Audit Office, 1993b, p. 11). At first this report created little publicity. However, during the subsequent parliamentary hearings of the report, questioning by members of the House of Commons Public Accounts Committee began to uncover the first threads of what subsequently became a highly publicized scandal involving not just the Overseas Aid Minister (who had evidently been overruled in the matter) but the Secretary of State for Defence, the Foreign Secretary, and then Prime Minister Thatcher. Evidently the aid for the dam had been used as a sweetener to the Malaysian government to help persuade them to buy a large quantity of British military hardware (see, for example, Hencke, 1994). Although the NAO's auditors must surely have uncovered some of the leads to this larger network of decisions, no reference to any of the other issues appeared on the surface of the report. The report stuck narrowly to the procedural question of whether the aid conformed to the aid guidelines and whether the financing for the project had been fashioned in the most economical way. As to the larger issue, it concluded: "It is not for the National Audit office to question the merits of this policy decision" (National Audit Office, 1993b, p. 11). It was left to the politicians on the Public Accounts Committee to read this signpost and then promptly begin to ask more political questions.

Professional no-go areas are perhaps less clearly marked. Bold SAIs can and do penetrate professional territories, usually with relevant professionals co-opted onto their teams. For example, the NAO was able to report on clinical audit (National Audit Office, 1994a) and the Audit Commission has tackled a whole series of topics of great sensitivity to both the teaching and medical professions.

On the whole, the SAO seems to have been rather more cautious than either the NAO or the Audit Commission in their explorations of professional territory. Their emphasis has remained more exclusively on financial management, and has kept away from those issues of service quality that can prove particularly sensitive for public service professionals. In their recent medium-term plan, the SAO states very clearly, "The audited topic must always be approached from a financial point of view. Argumentation connected to this basic task of the SAO must be clearly explicated both in the definition of objectives and in the reporting of findings of each audit" (State Audit Office, 1995b, p. 2, translated from the Finnish original by Hilkka Summa).

Despite this tighter financial focus, the SAO sometimes comes up against vigorous professional criticism. When Finnish auditors found a record of declining productivity in Finnish prisons (a falling prison population but no fall in total resources consumed) it argued that this was connected with the lack of any effectiveness measures among the prisons' existing performance indicators and prepared itself to recommend that new measures of outcomes (proxied by rates of recidivism) should be installed. However, the prison service pointed out that recidivism rates depended principally on factors beyond their control, such as employment opportunities, family support, friendship networks, health, and so on. The Department of Prison Administration therefore resisted the proposed emphasis on recidivism and instead developed a set of process-oriented indicators such as physical conditions in the prisons, range of services available, and so on (Summa, 1996).

In general, in relation to no-go territories, evaluators are in a weaker position than performance auditors. They lack statutory rights of access and must depend on the power of the commissioning authority (plus any general legislation on freedom of information that may exist in the country concerned). The tales of evaluators who have been thwarted by the unwillingness of state bodies to afford them access are legion. Independent academic researchers, in particular, may have little to offer ministries and agencies in return for access. They can therefore be regarded as a waste of time or, worse, a potential embarrassment. The willingness of many public bodies to submit voluntarily to independent investigation may well have diminished as, over the last two decades, time and cost pressures have increased and the luxury of talking to academics has been regarded as less and less justifiable (see, for example, Pollitt, Harrison, Hunter, and Marnoch, 1990). On the other hand, evaluators commissioned by a powerful sponsor (say a central ministry or department) to investigate a subordinate body (a state agency) may find themselves in a position more akin to that of an SAI auditor.

Selecting the Tools

Neither auditors nor evaluators can afford to rely principally on their impressionistic judgments. If their account is to carry authority, it must usually be based on the use of the tools or methods that are generally accepted as being appropriate for the topics under investigation.

In this regard, the advent of performance audit has certainly helped SAIs widen the range of tools that they commonly employ. The days when auditors simply came in and checked the books have long since passed (if they ever existed). For example, NAO reports of the last decade or so appear to be methodologically considerably more adventurous than those of the previous period. They include, inter alia, the use of customer satisfaction surveys for national museums and for the issuance of driving licenses (National Audit Office, 1993d, 1993e), surveys of opinion among participants in government subsidy schemes (National Audit Office, 1991, 1994a), and construction of economic models showing estimates of displacement, deadweight, and additionality for a system of regional subsidies (National Audit Office, 1991). Similarly, the SAO conducts statistical sampling and employs a range contemporary analytical techniques.

Thus a reading of almost a hundred NAO reports from 1993 through 1995 revealed use of a wide range of tools and techniques, most of which might equally have been used by evaluators working on the same topics. Insofar as this review revealed differences with the armamentarium typical of evaluation reports, these were not particularly striking. Three, though, are perhaps worthy of brief mention.

First, although SAIs undoubtedly use interviews quite extensively, they tend not to document these in quite the same way as might academic evaluators. Interview schedules are seldom published, the numbers and types and conditions of interview are frequently unrecorded. Problems of validating interview-derived data are not discussed. Second, SAIs appear to be slightly more cautious than evaluators about entering into comparative analysis that goes beyond the organizations immediately under investigation. The idea of comparing an activity in one organization to similar processes elsewhere comes very quickly to most social science–trained evaluators (and is fundamental to business techniques like benchmarking) but the NAO, in particular, seldom adopts this tactic. This may have something to do with problems of clearing the report at the final stage, as discussed later in this chapter. Third, SAI reports differ from academic evaluations in that they tend to make less reference (or none at all) to other work on the same or similar topics. A typical academic evaluation will be festooned with references to other studies and may well include some kind of formal literature review. Such papers convey a sense of the evaluators adding to some cumulative and collective body of knowledge and insight. SAI reports read more as stand-alone products.

While we would defend our broad conclusion that the tool kits resorted to by performance auditors and evaluators extensively overlap, this observation requires one further, significant qualification. While individual tools may be taken up and used by either performance auditors or evaluators, the process within which they are selected and applied may be significantly different. This point may be encapsulated by referring to the subheading of the previous section—"Planning and Design." Several auditors have told us that their internal processes of setting up the performance audit may be described as planning but seldom amounts to design. Designing a study would be much more common in the world of evaluation, where there is a greater degree of self-consciousness about the way the different methodological components articulate together and about their individual and collective adequacy in relation to the particular evaluatory questions that the study is seeking to address. In good evaluations, therefore, individual instruments will be very carefully related to their expected method of application, which will in turn be considered alongside the selection and application of other tools, the entire ensemble being conceived as an overall design. This particular way of thinking may not be entirely unknown in SAI audit teams, but it seems as yet comparatively rare. More commonly, audit teams will plan their audits in a fairly pragmatic fashion, selecting on a more-or-less ad hoc basis whatever tools and methods seem potentially useful for shedding light on the chosen program or institution.

Delays

SAIs have to sustain their investigations in the field through what may become quite extended periods. During this time auditees may be more or less cooperative. They may be tardy in producing requested information and slow to arrange meetings. As the final report begins to be drafted, they may raise a host of detailed objections not only to the facts but to the ways in which the auditors have framed and expressed particular issues (see, for example, Roberts and Pollitt, 1994, p. 534). Most SAIs lay considerable stress on checking their facts with auditees (what evaluators sometimes term *respondent validation*), but the auditees may produce ingeniously restrictive definitions of what constitutes the dividing line between facts and mere opinions. Patience is frequently a useful quality in an auditor.

SAIs can thus quite frequently find themselves with slippage on their intended completion dates, but evaluators are probably even more exposed to delay. Their terms of reference may be modified in midstudy, as the interests of the commissioning authority shift with current political tides. They may encounter recalcitrant evaluees who simply refuse to talk to them, or even lobby the commissioners to get them removed. Powerful ministers may reject the very need to evaluate their pet reforms (Robinson and Le Grand, 1994, p. 1). The advisability of confirming factual information is only one entry on a long list of potential delays.

Which Information Is Usable?

One important feature of any audit is thus the *clearance* arrangements through which an audit team checks out its draft report with the auditees. The precise rules and understandings around this vary significantly among different SAIs. The NAO is quite conservative. Although not obliged to do so by statute, they clear each report, line by line, with the audited body. This is mainly because the NAO has an agreement with the Parliamentary Public Accounts Committee (the organization they serve) to the effect that they will only submit agreed texts to Parliament. Several auditors have told us that the knowledge that this process will have to be gone through at the end of the expedition causes them to think very carefully before embarking on a line of investigation that could be deemed even remotely speculative, untypical, or critically comparative with other bodies beyond the strict scope of the investigation.

Though very careful to check its material with professionals and other representatives of audited bodies, the Audit Commission seems less inhibited in this regard. Of course, it does not have to submit its reports for parliamentary scrutiny and debate, and therefore does not labor under the same "no disagreements about the facts" convention as does the NAO.

Like other SAIs, the SAO offers auditees an opportunity to contest draft findings. Unlike the NAO, where disagreement often seems to be excluded or fudged, SAO reports may explicitly include auditee comments in the text, so that the final report proceeds on a thesis-antithesis-synthesis basis. In general, it would appear that auditors at the SAO are somewhat less constrained than those at the NAO in terms of freedom to write their own reports in their own words.

Like auditors, evaluators may frequently find themselves the repositories of anecdotal and other information that cannot be embodied in their final report. This will be particularly true for evaluators working within hard, primarily quantitative designs (such as most economic evaluations). For those employing pluralistic or naturalistic assumptions matters may be somewhat less constricted. Reporting (often called *sharing*) fears, feelings, and perceptions is very much part of the function of the "fourth generation" evaluator, whereas this is precisely the type of information an auditor will inevitably encounter but feel obliged to exclude from the report—unless, perhaps, it can be given the scientific status of a survey. As a generalization, it might be said that while value analysis and cognitive mapping stand as accepted parts of pluralistic evaluation, performance auditors usually avoid information of that type.

Does the Final Report Make an Impact?

Finally, the auditors arrive back at base, having cleared their story with the auditees. It can at last be released to the wider public. However, its impact will often depend partly on the chance factor of what other news is current at that particular time. If the topic the auditors set off to investigate (sometimes long ago) is now fashionable, their report may have great public impact. If, however, the political and media spotlight has meanwhile moved on to other topics, then their report may have very little public effect. If a report comes out at a time when there is little other news, it may receive disproportionate attention—for example, at the time of writing (toward the end of a hot summer and during the political holiday period), a 1995 NAO report on the U.K. Meteorological Office was being favored with intense media attention (National Audit Office, 1995b). Because of this, there may be sensitive decisions to take both about the timing of the release of reports and about their slant or emphasis, and these may be taken by SAI top management rather than the members of the expedition themselves (for an example of this happening in the U.K. Audit Commission, see Henkel, 1991, pp. 40–43).

There may also be some tension between the requirements of different audiences. General politicians and the lay public may want a diet of dramatic stories—tales of waste, corruption, and inefficiency, replete with good guys and bad guys. However, the audited bodies themselves may respond best to careful, modulated presentations that make recommendations for nondramatic incremental improvements.

In all these respects, there is little difference between audit reports and evaluations. Both are at the mercy of the unpredictable movements of the political spotlight, and of the attentions of the mass media. Both SAIs and evaluation units need to think hard about how to strike a balance between, on one hand, generating popular interest and support and, on the other, convincing and enrolling insiders.

Performance Audit and Evaluation: What Is the Warrant for Their Recommendations?

Audit reports are supposed to make things better. They are supposed to be authoritative, unbiased, above mere political argument, objective, conclusive. This is a very demanding specification—many would say impossible—and the shift from old-fashioned financial audit to performance auditing has made these expectations more difficult than ever to meet.

The traditional audit criteria of procedural correctness have been supplemented by more complex (and slippery) criteria of economy, efficiency, effectiveness, and quality. The positivist myth that there is only one true story to be told is more and more obviously unsustainable. Whereas in traditional financial auditing, accounts are certified as constituting a true and fair account, no such epistemological claim is made on the surface of performance audits. As the British Comptroller and Auditor General has acknowledged: "there can be no such thing as an objective appraisal of whether a programme has a positive or a negative impact" (Bourn, 1992, p. 44).

More concretely, it is an interesting feature of most NAO VFM audits that their recommendations are not costed (and neither, quite frequently, are the improvements that the recommendations are intended to bring about). In effect, audited bodies are thus invited to undertake uncosted changes in pursuit of unestimated benefits. Not all SAIs operate in this way. The Audit Commission, for example, frequently provides estimates of potential savings if its recommendations were to be adopted. This is therefore another interesting point of internal diversity among SAIs. Nevertheless, where uncosted recommendations do occur, the authority of the SAI concerned is brought into sharp focus.

The issue might be summarized as follows: If SAIs have moved well beyond criteria of procedural accounting correctness yet frequently do not offer solid estimates of the costs and benefits of their recommendations, then what criteria are in play, and why should auditees pay the SAIs any heed? Inspection of NAO, Audit Commission, and SAO reports reveals a variety of audit criteria, both explicit and implicit. Not surprisingly, economy and efficiency are frequently mentioned, though not always operationally defined. Quality is a concept deployed in several recent NAO reports, and seems to be loosely equated with either customer satisfaction or good practice or both (National Audit Office, 1993d, 1993e, 1995). Quality also features in Audit Commission and SAO reports. Good practice is another criterion, and a particularly interesting one. It is seldom much explicated other than by reference to peer opinion (for example, National Audit Office, 1993c; Audit Commission, 1995). Thus performance auditors in SAIs are now operating far beyond their traditional sphere of competence as accountants. They have become interpreters of the expectations, objectives, good practice, and general principles of a range of other groups—policy makers, administrators, managers, and professionals.

In this context, our research has identified quite a few instances of SAI interpretations being vigorously contested—and effectively rejected—by the auditees, or by government ministers representing them. For example, there have been several cases where SAO reports have been criticized by Finnish politicians. In February 1995, an SAO report on the system for rating the financial capacity of municipalities suggested that the system was wasteful, inequitable, and in need of reform. The Minister of the Interior then arranged a press conference at which he accused the auditors of hindsight and of politicking by releasing the report close to the elections. The following month, the Minister of Transport also resorted to a press conference when he wanted to attack an SAO report that was critical of the prevailing system of subsidies to the shipping industry. It is noteworthy, however, that neither in these nor other cases has the auditor general reacted to the accusations or the SAO conclusions been changed.

These and other examples raise the question of the implicit model of feedback (or, more politically, influence) that underlies audit. As a senior Dutch auditor has pointed out, the model underlying traditional audit, and to some extent inherited by performance audit, is both mechanistic and naive (Leeuw, 1995). It apparently supposes that, once the audit team has reported:

- The auditee will read and listen to the recommendations.
- The auditee will take action to meet the recommendations.
- This action will lead to the realization of the formal goals of the audit.
- The action will not lead to any unintended or undesired side effects.

In such a model, auditors can retain their distance from the auditees. Unfortunately, it has few other virtues. In the real world, each assumption in the chain can be easily faulted, and the impact of performance audit thereby put in doubt.

Alternative models are readily available. They generally require greater efforts by the audit team to be seen as supportive of auditees and to negotiate and sell their recommendations, rather as do management consultants. The first steps toward such a relationship may be seen in a number of SAI practices, such as the SAO guidelines recommending that auditors enter into open dialogue with auditees (State Audit Office, 1995b). But insofar as such alternative models increase the probability of having an impact on auditee behavior, they decrease the distance between auditor and auditee. More interactive forms of reporting tend to work best when the parties are both closer to each other and more equal in status than SAIs have sometimes felt comfortable with vis à vis departments and agencies in the past.

These issues are familiar ones to students of evaluation. In the United States, early experimental paradigms of evaluation gave ground, during the 1970s and 1980s, to conceptions of the activity that stressed the need to convince audiences to use evaluation findings (Palumbo, 1988). It was more and more widely recognized that having a scientific basis alone was not enough to ensure that a piece of knowledge would actually be applied to solve problems and streamline operations (Lindblom and Cohen, 1979, pp. 40–42). Within the field of evaluation, the result has been the development of a more diverse and differentiated range of models that evaluators can offer their clients. Within audit, change has been slower to come, but there are now signs that SAIs are becoming more conscious of the need to convince and carry their audiences, not merely to be right.

Concluding Reflections

We are conscious that this chapter has not been able to give adequate attention to a number of the issues it has touched upon. In particular, there is scope for a much more systematic analysis of the differences we have noted *between* SAIs, and, indeed, for deeper exploration of the varied types of external education.

There are many similarities and shared contingencies between performance audit and evaluation. Both auditors and evaluators study formal documentation, carry out interviews with key decision makers, undertake surveys, hire expert consultants, draw on the findings of professional peer review, use economic concepts such as additionality, deadweight, and displacement, undertake statistical analysis, and so on. Indeed, it is hard to see that there is more than a marginal difference in the tool kits potentially available to performance auditors and evaluators.

Furthermore, evaluators usually need to negotiate access while auditors, though not obliged, commonly find it prudent to do so; both seek to avoid extensively antagonizing their subjects, consult over the nature of their final reports, and present these reports in ways that are likely to capture the attention of and convince their intended audiences. Both auditors and evaluators deploy argumentative and presentational skills and both—despite their ritualistic protestations to the contrary—frequently become political actors. We mean this not in the crude sense of advocating a particular doctrine or favoring a particular interest group, but as contributing to political agenda setting (through their choices of topics to investigate) and in framing the problems and issues in those areas (by implementing their particular methodological perspectives and modes of discourse).

However, there are also some very important differences between performance audit and external evaluation. The institutional homes from which audits and evaluations are launched, and to which they return, offer sharp contrasts. SAIs are generally rather august bodies. They house a coherent, well-defined professional community, buttressed by internationally accepted standards and formidable statutory powers. The home institution is acutely concerned with the way in which the findings of individual audits will reflect on the broader standing of the organization. Henkel stresses how the Audit Commission "must present itself as a national body fulfilling a significant mandate and possessing credentials to succeed" (Henkel, 1991, p. 63). A similar strong sense of institutional and collective solidarity was frequently manifest in our interviews with staff at both the NAO and the SAO.

Evaluation units can seldom if ever offer their staffs such a firmly founded (or firmly funded!) base for their studies. Their institutional histories are shorter, their statutory powers nonexistent, their staff less homogenous and more prone to rapid turnover. They have rivals and competitors in a sense that an SAI usually does not. Of course, evaluation units do their best to promote and defend their reputations, but their aspirations in this regard are frequently somewhat different from those of the SAIs. Evaluation units want to be known for good work, exciting ideas, original insights, clever staff, and—of course—influence (Weiss, 1992). The last-named is usually only achieved by getting close to political leaders or top officials—a procedure that, as we have seen, is still regarded with a degree of reserve by SAIs.

A further marked difference occurs in the processes of choosing topics and planning investigations. As we have seen, auditors have real, if not total, independence in regard to topic choice. This sets them apart from evaluation units, which are driven principally by what is demanded by those with the resources to commission studies. This severely constrains the areas that evaluators can penetrate, as does their limited ability (compared with SAIs armed with statutory mandates) to disperse the fog of official secrecy. The contrast is not absolute (a determined university evaluation team, working with pure academic funding, can get a long way) but we would argue that it is nonetheless significant.

In respect of the planning of investigations, despite overlapping tool kits, auditors and evaluators still represent different cultures. A theoretically and methodologically defensible design is of great importance to an evaluator. It is one of the main yardsticks against which peers will judge the work. Auditors, by contrast, need a practical plan to deliver a workmanlike report within a given time scale.

As one might expect, the differences back at base and in the ability to choose topics are reflected in the tone of the reports themselves. Performance auditors, notwithstanding their excursions beyond the comfortable world of verification, still wish to present their material as definitive, factual, and value-neutral. Furthermore, whatever the methodological foundation of performance audit, the emphasis of the published texts of SAIs is usually still—however politely—corrective. There is some variation here: Audit Commission reports on the whole perhaps tend to read as rather more user friendly than those of the NAO or SAO. Nevertheless, auditors are seldom genuine exponents of formative or supportive assessments. Their first priority is rarely that of helping the staff working to deliver a particular program or project.

In short, helping the auditee may be a secondary objective—even an important one—but it is pursued only insofar as it can be reconciled with the primary purpose of public accountability. This prime focus cannot be abandoned without also abandoning the most distinctive feature of SAIs—their unique statutory authority as agents of democratic transparency and accountability.

Evaluators, by contrast, can seldom occupy the democratic high ground. They lack the statutory authority (and often also the independence) of SAIs and must distinguish their reports on a different basis. Their claim is less one of special authority than of superior methodology and expertise. Their analyses should be believed because they are more carefully put together than other accounts—by experts. Their answers may not be the right answers, but they are more rigorous, defensible, or creative answers than anyone else's. The evaluatory methodology may be scientific or naturalistic, but in either case it is self-consciously displayed and defended as the most appropriate for the particular circumstances. The prime emphasis is less one of correction than of exploration—probing causal and correlational relationships in ways that may stimulate program shapers and implementors to approach familiar issues in a new light (scientific approaches) or mapping stakeholders' perceptions, expectations, and tolerances in the hope of finding common ground (naturalistic approaches).

Finally, a brief thought-experiment may illustrate our central point. Suppose that, while examining the same topic, an SAI and a commissioned, external evaluation unit accidentally published exactly the same text. (This is improbable, given the SAIs' discussed predilections for an authoritative, corrective style, but we ask readers momentarily to suspend disbelief.) Would the significance and reception of the reports then be the same? Our provisional answer is no. A report must always exist within and derive some of its significance from the particular context in which it is read. Despite convergent tool kits, SAIs and external evaluation units tell their tales from different positions in the networks of power relationships.

Acknowledgments

We are grateful for comments from our colleagues at Brunel University—David Burningham, Mary Henkel, Tim Packwood, and Simon Roberts. Eleanor Chelimsky also contributed some insightful remarks. We wish to acknowledge the helpfulness of staff at the NAO in London and the SAO in Helsinki. The responsibility for the opinions expressed in this chapter is, of course, ours alone.

References

Audit Commission. *Towards Better Management of Secondary Education.* London: Audit Commission, 1986.

Audit Commission. *Critical Path: An Analysis of Pathology Service.* London: Audit Commission, 1993.

Audit Commission. *Setting the Records Straight: A Study of Hospital Medical Records.* London: Audit Commission, 1995.

Bourn, J. "Evaluating the Performance of Central Government." In C. Pollitt and S. Harrison (eds.), *Handbook of Public Services Management.* Oxford, England: Blackwell Business, 1992.

Chelimsky, E. "Comparing and Contrasting Auditing and Evaluation: Some Notes on Their Relationship." *Evaluation Review,* 1985, *9* (4), 483–503.

Comptroller and Auditor General. *National Audit Office Programme for 1993–94 and Areas for Consideration for 1994–95.* Memorandum by the Comptroller and Auditor General. London: House of Commons, 1993.

Dekker, P., and Leeuw, F. "Program Evaluation and Effectiveness Auditing: Definitions, Models and Practice." In H. Becker and D. van Krefeld (eds.), *Program Evaluation.* Utrecht: van Arkel, 1989.

Greenberg, D., and Mandell, M. ["Research Utilization in Policy Making: A Tale of Two Series (of Social Experiments)."] *Journal of Policy Analysis and Management,* 1991, *10* (4), 633–656.

Guba, E., and Lincoln, Y. *Fourth Generation Evaluation.* Thousand Oaks, Calif.: Sage, 1989.

Hellstern, G.-M. "Generating Knowledge and Refining Experience: The Task of Evaluation." In F. Kaufman (ed.), *The Public Sector: Challenge for Co-ordination and Learning.* Hawthorne, N.Y.: Aldine de Gruyter, 1991.

Hencke, D. "Thatcher's Secret Arms Deal: Malaysia Offered Cheap Loans." *Guardian,* Feb. 16, 1994, p. 1.

Henkel, M. *Evaluation, Government and Change.* London: Jessica Kingsley, 1991.

Leeuw, F. L. "Performance Auditing, New Public Management, and Performance Improvement: Questions and Challenges." *Accounting, Auditing and Accountability,* forthcoming.

Lindblom, C., and Cohen, D. *Usable Knowledge: Social Science and Social Problem-Solving.* New Haven, Conn.: Yale University Press, 1979.

Longdon, P. "A Case Study in Performance Auditing: The Audit Commission (England and Wales)." Paper presented to the Public Management Service, OECD, Symposium on Performance Auditing and Performance Improvement in Government, Paris, June 1995.

National Audit Office. *Creating and Safeguarding Jobs in Wales.* London: Her Majesty's Stationery Office, 1991.

National Audit Office. *Progress on the Department of Transport's Motorway Widening Programme, HC10.* London: Her Majesty's Stationery Office, 1993a.

National Audit Office. *Pergau Hydro-electric Project, HC908.* London: Her Majesty's Stationery Office, 1993b.

National Audit Office. *Repeat Prescribing by General Medical Practitioners in England, HC897.* London: Her Majesty's Stationery Office, 1993c.

National Audit Office. *The Driving and Vehicle Licensing Agency: Quality of Service to Customers, HC105.* London: Her Majesty's Stationery Office, 1993d.

National Audit Office. *Department of National Heritage, National Museums and Galleries: Quality of Service to the Public, HC841.* London: Her Majesty's Stationery Office, 1993e.

National Audit Office. *The Renewable Energy Research, Development and Administration Programme, HC156.* London: Her Majesty's Stationery Office, 1994a.

National Audit Office. *Ministry of Defence: Management of the Trident Works Programme, HC621.* London: Her Majesty's Stationery Office, 1994b.

National Audit Office. *Annual Report 1994.* London: National Audit Office, 1994c.

National Audit Office. *Ministry of Defence: Defence Procurement in the 1990s, HC390.* London: Her Majesty's Stationery Office, 1994d.

National Audit Office, *Clinical Audit in England, HC27.* London: Her Majesty's Stationery Office, 1995a.

National Audit Office. *The Meteorological Office Executive Agency: Evaluation of Performance, HC693.* London: Her Majesty's Stationery Office, 1995b.

Palumbo, D. (ed.). *The Politics of Program Evaluation.* Thousand Oaks, Calif.: Sage, 1988.

Pollitt, C. "Occasional Excursions: A Brief History of Policy Evaluation in the UK." *Parliamentary Affairs,* 1993, *46* (3), 353–362.

Pollitt, C., Harrison, S., Hunter, D. J., and Marnoch, G. "No Hiding Place: On the Discomforts of Researching the Contemporary Policy Process." *Journal of Social Policy,* 1990, *19* (2), 169–190.

Power, M. *The Audit Explosion.* London: Demos, 1994.

Rist, R. C. "Management Accountability: The Signals Sent by Auditing and Evaluation." *Journal of Public Policy,* 1989, *9* (3), 355–369.

Roberts, S., and Pollitt, C. "Audit or Evaluation? A National Audit Office Value-for-Money Study." *Public Administration,* 1994, *72* (4), 527–549.

Robinson, R., and Le Grand, J. *Evaluating the NHS Reforms.* London: King's Fund Institute, 1994.

Shadish, W., Cook, T., and Leviton, L. *Foundations of Program Evaluation: Theories of Practice.* Thousand Oaks, Calif: Sage, 1991.

Sloan, N. *Performance Audit and Other Evaluative Studies Compared.* Unpublished master of philosophy thesis, Brunel University, 1995.

State Audit Office. *Teollisuuden tutkimus—ja tuotekehitystoiminnan edistaminen, Valtiontalouden tarkastusvirasto* [Audit Report on State Subsidies to Industry for Technology and Product Development]. Tarkastuskertomus nro 291/54/90. Helsinki: State Audit Office, 1991.

State Audit Office. *Annual Report: the State Audit Office of Finland.* Helsinki: State Audit Office, Painatuskeskus Oy, 1995a.

State Audit Office. *Valtiontalouden tarkastusviraston toiminta—ja taloussuunnitelma vuosille 1996–1999* [State Audit Office Plan of Action and Finances for 1996–1999], VTV 260/20/95, 21st Apr. Helsinki: 1995b.

Summa, H. "Giving Up Orthodoxy in Performance Measurement: From Effectiveness to Process Measures in the Case of Finnish Prison Administration." In A. Halachmi and D. Grant (eds.), *Performance Measurement and Re-engineering in Criminal Justice and Social Programs.* Perth: Ministry of Justice, Western Australia, 1996.

Weiss, C. (ed.). *Organizations for Policy Analysis: Helping Government Think.* Thousand Oaks, Calif.: Sage, 1992.

CHRISTOPHER POLLITT *is dean of the Faculty of Social Sciences, Brunel University, United Kingdom.*

HILKKA SUMMA *is a counselor with the Ministry of Finance, Finland.*

This chapter describes differences and similarities between auditing and evaluation and their respective contributions to performance improvement.

Auditing and Evaluation: Bridging a Gap, Worlds to Meet?

Frans L. Leeuw

Papers in which differences and similarities of auditing and evaluation are discussed appear every now and then in academic journals (Chelimsky, 1985; Walker, 1985; Rist, 1989; Leeuw, 1992). Sometimes the perspective taken is methodological (for example, differences in techniques of data gathering and analysis), sometimes differences and similarities in scope are discussed. There are also papers in which differences in the institutional position of audits versus evaluations are discussed.

In this chapter I will discuss the contributions of auditors and evaluators toward performance improvement. This perspective is crucial because national audit institutions and internal audit organizations have increasingly formulated their mission not only to assess and contribute to accountability of the public sector, but also to improve the performance of this sector. Evaluators have long had such a mission.

The second reason for choosing this perspective is that, at least in Western Europe and North America, auditees more and more expect a hands-on approach from auditors and evaluators. By auditing I mean traditional financial audit, compliance audit, and performance audit. These activities all focus on the adequacy of information and the systems that produce this information (Public Management Group/Organization for Economic Coordination and Development, 1995). By evaluation I mean program and policy evaluations in which goal achievement and the intended and unintended side effects of policies and programs are central dependent variables.

First, I describe some characteristics of auditing and evaluation. Next, the contributions of auditing to improvement of the public sector are discussed, while the same is done for evaluations. Finally, some suggestions are formulated on how to handle the intricate relationships between auditing, evaluation, and performance improvement.

Needless to say, what follows is a broad and somewhat stylized description based on my understanding of the situation, primarily in Western Europe.

Some Characteristics of Audits

In identifying audit characteristics, it is wise to start with a consideration of which types of variables are central.

Variables Investigated. Central in auditing is the role played by financial managers responsible for the policy or organization audited. Day and Klein (1987, p. 26) refer to "managerial accountability," which "is about making those with delegated authority answerable for carrying out agreed tasks according to agreed criteria of performance." Management therefore is one of the core variables, or clusters of variables, in a performance audit.

Also within the core of an audit is the analysis of the relationship between public expenditures and policy instruments. Audits are fundamentally linked with governmental receipts and expenses, often grounded in statute. The audit not only aims to present new findings, but especially strives to judge the efficiency and effectiveness of management. This necessitates emphasis on formally pinning down the objectives of the policy instrument under investigation. Auditors tend to be rather strongly concerned with legal and procedural compliance issues.

Methods and Techniques Applied. Auditors are usually greatly concerned that evidence comes from authoritative sources such as the chief executives of ministries and agencies. Empirical evidence from mail, telephone, or face-to-face surveys usually is not enough foundation for auditors' judgments so the analysis and conclusions rely heavily on documentary evidence.

A multimethod or triangulated approach is usually only applied in large-scale performance audits. Also, advanced statistical techniques are not often applied, nor is attention usually paid to methods of argumentation analysis (for example, assumptional analysis).

Underlying Concept of Auditing. Moukheibir and Barzelay (1995) have identified some underlying concepts and assumptions of auditing. This approach can be linked to earlier studies by Mason and Mitroff (1981) on analyzing strategic planning assumptions, work by Chen (1990) on theories-in-action underlying policy programs, and to Leeuw (1992) on articulating and evaluating "policy theories."

Moukheibir and Barzelay (1995, pp. 3–6) reconstruct the model that underlies traditional financial audit—the theory that the government resembles a machine bureaucracy. This bureaucracy is thought to function well when officials apply legal norms and technical standards to matters within their assigned areas of authority and responsibility. "The role orientation of the organizations that conduct traditional audits is to be institutionally aloof, or independent, from both political authorities and bureaucracy."

The performance audit is based on the theory that government acts as an "adaptive organism: this image portrays managers as agents performing important functions, including adapting organizations to shifts in their mandates and resources. . . . The concept of performance audit is characterized primarily by the view that the public sector functions well when managerial rationality is applied to the perennial task of adjusting means to ends and, in particular, to accomplishing results with resources" (Moukheibir and Barzelay, 1995, p. 5). Here the role orientation is to that of independence and to rendering judgments about the design and operation of governmental organizations.

Some Characteristics of Evaluations

The variables and methods employed by evaluators are often quite different from those of auditors.

Variables Investigated. Evaluators are involved in studying the actual implementation of policy programs and instruments in society (on site and in depth). "Evaluation researchers have tended to avoid management issues until the past 10–15 years. The emergence of the program implementation literature was in response to the tendency to focus on program impact measurement while treating programs as unexamined 'black boxes'" (Davis, 1990, p. 37). Evaluators are not primarily interested in obtaining data only from managers responsible for the implementation of policies or programs, but instead on gathering data through fieldwork.

Usually, audits are strongly focused on assessing the economy and efficiency of expenditures made on behalf of policies, but evaluations are not. A social policy researcher evaluating subsidies will not analyze variables such as the relative success or failure of cash control mechanisms or the effects of budgetary principles. However, policy evaluations focusing on cost-effectiveness methods are linked with financial issues.

"Evaluation tries to understand the program objectives but does not require auditing precision in them, since program effectiveness is not necessarily measured against objectives. Evaluation is more interested in measuring the changes observed after the program was introduced, and in comparing these changes with what would have happened without the program" (Chelimsky, 1990, p. 51).

Evaluators often analyze at least two theories. One theory—the explanatory theory—refers to hypotheses used by the evaluator to explain findings from the investigation. The other—the policy theory—refers to the reconstructed set of assumptions that underlies the policy or program under review and that specifies the social and behavioral mechanisms behind the success or failure of the policy.

Methods and Techniques Applied. Data collection relies heavily on quantitative and qualitative methods and on techniques stemming from the social and behavioral sciences (for example: interviews, questionnaires, and observation). Often data are collected at the grassroots level of society. Evaluation researchers often make use of a number of simultaneously applied statistical techniques, the multimethod approach.

Underlying Concept of Evaluations. The underlying concept is that government functions well when its programs (seen as clinical interventions) are subject to scientific scrutiny and more or less pass the examination. "Governments are successful when the effectiveness of treatments (= interventions) increases" (Moukheibir and Barzelay, 1995, p. 4). This image of governmental functioning helps to sanction the goal orientation of program evaluators. That is "to empirically test hypotheses, embedded within policy arguments. . . . The role orientation of the program evaluator is to be a kind of policy scientist."

Improving Public Sector Performance Through Auditing

In Western Europe and North America, the concept of New Public Management (NPM) is popular (for a similar concept, see Osborne and Gaebler's *Reinventing Government* [1992]). It emphasizes economy, efficiency, and effectiveness of governmental organizations, policy instruments, and policy programs. NPM strives for a greater quality of service delivery and for an improvement of the functioning of the public sector. Less attention is paid to compliance with formally prescribed processes, rules, and procedures. Other goals of NPM are: loosening controls and devolving greater responsibility to operating managers, creating additional flexibility or autonomy for managers, making public sector managers manage, and putting a greater focus on risk management and performance measurement (Public Management Group/Organization for Economic Coordination and Development, 1995, pp. 9–10).

When auditors study NPM, they are usually interested in topics such as the extent to which regularity and compliance with the law will be jeopardized due to the devolvement of management responsibilities. Another concern is with the quality and quantity of accountability information produced by NPM officials. Are there plans, procedures, monitoring devices, evaluation infrastructures, and the like?

Yet another topic of interest to auditors is the level of goal achievement by the NPM. Will the goals set by NPM indeed be realized? Striving for performance improvement of governments is not equal to realizing improvement. Studies on intended and unintended consequences of policy making show that goals sometimes run the risk of being so promising and challenging that politicians and bureaucrats, merely by publicly stressing their importance, believe that they are already realized.

Auditing and Improving Public Sector Performance. A crucial mission of auditing—contributing to the improvement of the public sector—corresponds to a central goal of the New Public Management. Therefore, one might assume that NPM officials would welcome auditors. However, in practice things are not that simple. It appears that the relationship between auditing and NPM is not without difficulties.

What are some of these difficulties? The fault-finding approach of auditors may be too narrow-minded and the auditors' lack of constructive suggestions may make the relationship between NPM and auditing difficult (Public Management Group/Organization for Economic Coordination and Development, 1995).

Smith (1995) mentions another difficulty—that performance measures can inhibit innovation and lead to ossification and organizational paralysis brought about by an excessively rigid system of measurement. Based on recent Dutch experiences, auditors are sometimes confronted with the question of why they don't pay attention to the negative impact of their fault-finding approach on the audited organization's human and social capital. Sometimes the commitment of employees to an organization declines after a performance audit is published, even when the findings of the report cover only side-aspects of the organization. This in turn may reduce the motivation of the employees.

Another difficulty stems from the love of auditors for procedures. Often attention is paid to the procedural and organizational prerequisites for an effective policy or an effective public organization. It is believed that when these prerequisites are met, the policy or the organization itself is effective.

Stressing procedural effectiveness has at least one other important side effect—tunnel vision. "Tunnel vision can be defined as an emphasis on phenomena that are quantified in the performance measurement scheme at the expense of unquantified aspects of performance. For example, maternity service managers in the United Kingdom's National Heath Service are increasingly being held to account by a single performance indicator, the perinatal mortality rate. There is clear evidence that the emphasis on the quantifiable mortality rate is distorting the nature of maternity services to the detriment of the nonquantifiable objectives" (Smith, 1995, p. 284).

Frey and Serna (1990) have enlarged the discussion, adding the topic of counterproductive consequences of auditing practices. Their study referred to national audit offices in Central European countries like Austria. They linked the quasi-monopolistic nature of audit offices with the production of procedural and formal information on performance. One of their arguments was that while this information may be needed from a legal perspective, it is counterproductive when viewed from the perspective of performance improvement.

These descriptions are examples of unintended and negative consequences of stressing procedural effectiveness. They also reflect the general difficulties of developing good performance measures. Auditors may stress the use of performance measures because they believe that the single, quantifiable indicator is generally an adequate proxy for effective programs. Sometimes, however, this is not true.

Links Between Characteristics and Difficulties of Auditing. To what extent are the foregoing difficulties in the relation between auditing and improvement of the public sector and the NPM linked to the characteristics of auditing described earlier? I believe there is a link. Due to the fact that traditional audit focuses on specific managerial variables and not on social or behavioral mechanisms, there is a strong attraction to rules and regulations and to making recommendations for improving rules and regulations. The fact that the multi-method approach is not often used may increase this inclination. The underlying concept of auditing is also a fertile soil for procedural recommendations.

Let me expand somewhat on this point and refer to the auditors' implicit feedback theory (Leeuw, forthcoming). This feedback theory can be stated as follows:

- Feedback from the auditor to the auditee is needed when it is shown that the standards or goals are not reached, or are inefficiently reached.
- The auditee will listen to the feedback.
- The auditee will take follow-up action.
- The follow-up action will lead to the realization of the formal goals.
- There will be no unintended and undesired side effects.

This theory assumes that the auditee refrains from strategic action (that is, action merely to make himself look good), which he *could* take because he is familiar with the standards or measurements that auditors apply. The theory also assumes that the likelihood of unintended and undesired side effects is small to zero.

What can be said about the empirical content or validity of this audit feedback theory? Meyer and O'Shaugnessy (1993) have recently presented evidence that strategic behavior does appear to be related to performance measurement. They explain this result using the concept of *isomorphism*. Standards and performance measurement stimulate strategic response behavior that creates an isomorphism—observance of the standards is mimicked but real performance may not be improved. Meyer and O'Shaugnessy stress that not only managers run the risk of mimicry, but also auditors, financial analysts, and evaluators.

Therefore, I believe that auditors who want to contribute to the improvement of the public sector should pay more attention to these underlying concepts—they should focus less on procedures and more on content.

Improving Public Sector Performance Through Evaluations

Evaluators are interested in NPM for a number of reasons. First, innovations like NPM always run the risk of mimicry. Early adopters of NPM may implement the philosophy in practice and indeed create successes, but other organizations start to imitate their successful predecessors without, however, realizing the same effects. Put somewhat differently—the later implementing organizations may have the form right (isomorphism), but the substance wrong. Legitimation has become more important than innovation. Evaluation research is able to unravel these different aspects of the implementation and adoption of NPM.

Second, implementing NPM runs the risk of leading to unintended and undesired consequences that are counterproductive to the formulated goals. Evaluation can unravel intended and unintended consequences. In the literature, examples of unintended consequences are given. One is *cream skimming,* that is, "discrimination by either purchasers or providers against the more expensive [program] users: the chronically-ill patient; the incontinent, confused, elderly person; the disruptive child . . . if purchasers can choose for whom they will purchase and providers can choose for whom they will provide, that is, if they can skim off the cream, then welfare services may not reach those who need them most and equity will not be achieved" (Le Grand and Bartlett, 1993, p. 32). This example stresses the importance of having clear performance measures.

Third, evaluators are interested in the implicit or underlying theory of NPM: why is it believed that delegating functions to quasi-autonomous non-governmental organizations— *quango-cratization* in the current jargon—or to private businesses, or the establishment of policy networks indeed will lead to a more effective and efficient public sector? Is it true that a leaner government means a stronger one? And is it true that public-private partnerships with very complex property rights indeed will lead to performance improvement?

Evaluation and Improving Public Sector Performance

Several difficulties must be overcome if evaluations are to lead to improvements in public performance. Some of them are now discussed.

What Are Some of the Difficulties? *Debatable and questionable results of evaluations.* This is caused by the pluralist conception of what distinguishes adequate from inadequate evaluations. Although meta-evaluations reduce this problem somewhat, government officials are still able to find both very positive and very negative reviews of one and the same evaluation report. Consensus on the level of epistemology has not yet been achieved. This reduces the likelihood that evaluations will make the public sector function better.

The love for "pragmatic evaluations." Pawson and Tilley (1995) indicate that the assumption underlying the pragmatic evaluation concept is that evaluation research methods are best learned through exemplars that involve skill, sensitivity, discipline, clarity, creativity, competence, and care. In this view, "truth is less important than servicing the practical business of policy making. The problem with pragmatism is that it denies any distinctive authority to evaluation. It becomes will o'the wisp. It looks good, because it is made to look good. . . . Because it ingratiates, pragmatic evaluation may win popularity" (pp. 24, 29).

The love for "naturalistic evaluations." Guba and Lincoln (1989) are the main architects and adherents of this approach. In accordance with the naturalistic way of construing social life, social programs are conceived of as processes involving negotiation between all those touched by and touching the work (Pawson and Tilley, 1995). The method involves finding these stakeholders, establishing their (not the researchers') constructions of the programs

via a prolonged period of observation, arranging for these claims to be nego-
tiated in a hermeneutic dialectical circle, and so forth.

First, one may ask what can be learnt from naturalistic evaluations. Will
the different reconstructions of different stakeholders not vary widely with
diverging interests, leading to nothing more than pictures of everybody's different interests? Second, as Pawson and Tilley (1995, p. 26) argue correctly,
this approach "misconceives the social world by overlooking pervasive power
asymmetries and social realities." Social reality is more than negotiating.

Finally, naturalistic evaluations make it impossible to believe in the added
value of quasi-experimental, natural science–oriented evaluations focusing on
unraveling effects of—for example—negative income transfer programs, family planning communication programs for teenagers (Udry, 1974), or sex education programs.

Links Between Characteristics and Difficulties of Evaluations. Pragmatic and naturalistic evaluations run a risk opposite that of auditing in terms
of the attention paid to rules, regulations, documentary evidence, and the like.
They almost deny the importance of these variables in decision processes in
the public sector. They forget that, when it boils down to implementing policy instruments and programs, legislators want to have information relevant
from the perspective of accountability.

Another problem is that NPM officials often have no time to lose. Numerous social and administrative problems have to be solved. Getting involved in
dialectical debates on the social constructions of the social problems usually isn't
favored by the electorate, nor will such debates solve the problems to be solved.

A final problem deals with the underlying concept of evaluations as reconstructed by Moukheibir and Barzelay (1995)—the idea that government functions well when the programs are subject to scientific scrutiny and more or less
pass the examination. This approach, not to be found in the realms of naturalistic evaluations but in the quasi-experimental approach, runs the risk of
focusing too much on what is technically and methodologically sound, for-
getting about the real questions of life. It may even lead to a variant on Gre-
sham's law—government activities that are evaluable in terms of quasi-
experimental designs will always drive out activities that are important but not
measurable (Wilson, 1989).

Some Final Remarks

How to solve some of the difficulties referred to? Briefly, here are some suggestions for discussion. A first task for auditors would be to develop and help implement performance measurement schemes that do not run the risks of tunnel
vision, fault-finding, and the like. Maybe one of Smith's recommendations is useful here (Smith, 1995, p. 304). He suggests involving "staff at all levels in the
development and implementation of performance measurement schemes." When
one applies this idea to the world of auditing, it may lead to a greater and more
open communication between auditors and NPM auditees on the criteria applied.

A second task may be to replace the implicit feedback theory of auditing by a more advanced theory of organizational learning (Argyris, 1982). It will probably enhance the likelihood that audit work will contribute substantially to the improvement of performance. Recent evidence from a comparative study on organizational learning and evaluation research corroborates this assumption (Leeuw, Rist, and Sonnichsen, 1994). This study shows that program evaluation contributes to single- and double-loop learning. Argyris (1982, p. 15) defines organizational learning as a "process of detecting and correcting error." It is a process in which an organization continually attempts to become competent in taking action, while at the same time reflecting on the action it takes to learn from its present and past efforts. This conceptual approach differentiates learning that occurs in single-or double-loop modes. Problem solving that enables an organization to better carry out its present policies and achieve its current objectives is defined as *single-loop learning*. A more comprehensive and systemic learning process occurs when *double-loop learning* comes into play. In this case, the assumptions underlying the policies and goals of a program are questioned, leading to the possibility of securing new, innovative, and permanent solutions to problems.

A third challenge is how to improve the training of auditors and open their minds for social and behavioral mechanisms operating in the public sector and in decision making. Government is for the people, but it also is a people's business. This is true for NPM officials as well as for auditors and evaluators. Therefore, training and education are crucial (Bemelmans-Videc, Eriksen, and Goldenberg, 1994).

Reducing pluralism in evaluation research as opposed to increasing pluralism in auditing is the fourth challenge I suggest for this profession. Investing more in meta-evaluations and in distinguishing the sheep from the goats should have high priority over the next years in evaluations.

Finally, I believe that combining the strong points of evaluation (the methodology applied and the attention paid to theories and theory-driven evaluations) with the strong points of auditing (the orientation toward management, the focus on following the money, and the attention paid to documentary evidence) may well lead to a new interdiscipline in the twenty-first century. If one takes into account the ages of the disciplines—the auditing profession has only reached middle age and the evaluation branch is still in its twenties—such a blending of the best out of two worlds is probably advantageous for theory, research, and practice. It is to be hoped that organizations like the American, Canadian, and European Evaluation Societies can help stimulate this process.

References

Argyris, C. *Reasoning, Learning, and Action: Individual and Organizational.* San Francisco: Jossey-Bass, 1982.

Bemelmans-Videc, M. L., Eriksen, B., and Goldenberg, E. N. "Facilitating Organizational Learning: Human Resource Management and Program Evaluation." In F. L. Leeuw, R. C. Rist, and R. C. Sonnichsen (eds.), *Can Governments Learn?* New Brunswick, N.J.: Transaction, 1994.

Chelimsky, E. "Comparing and Contrasting Auditing and Evaluation: Some Notes on Their Relationship." *Evaluation Review,* 1985, *9* (4), 483–503.

Chelimsky, E. "Expanding GAO's Capabilities in Program Evaluation." *The GAO Journal,* Winter/Spring 1990, *8,* p. 51.

Chen, H. *Theory-Driven Evaluations.* Thousand Oaks, Calif.: Sage, 1990.

Davis, D. F. "Do You Want a Performance Audit or a Program Evaluation?" *Public Administration Review,* 1990, *50,* 35–41.

Day, P., and Klein, D. *Accountabilities: Five Public Services.* New York: Tavistock, 1987.

Frey, B., and Serna, A. "Eine politisch-ökonomische Betrachtung des Rechnungshofs." *Finanzarchiv,* 1990, *48,* 244–270.

Guba, E., and Lincoln, Y. *Fourth Generation Evaluation.* Thousand Oaks, Calif.: Sage, 1989.

Leeuw, F. L. "Performance Auditing and Policy Evaluation: Discussing Similarities and Dissimilarities." *Canadian Journal of Program Evaluation,* 1992, *7,* 53–68.

Leeuw, F. L. "Performance Auditing, New Public Management, and Performance Improvement: Questions and Challenges." *Accounting, Auditing and Accountability,* forthcoming.

Leeuw, F. L., Rist, R. C., and Sonnichsen, R. C. (eds.). *Can Governments Learn?* New Brunswick, N.J.: Transaction, 1994.

LeGrand, J., and Bartlett, W. (eds.). *Quasi-Markets and Social Policy.* Old Tappan, N.J.: Macmillan, 1993.

Mason, R., and Mitroff, I. *Challenging Strategic Planning Assumptions.* New York: Wiley, 1981.

Moukheibir, C., and Barzelay, M. "Performance Auditing: Concept and Controversies." Paper presented at the Public Management Group/Organization for Economic Coordination and Development Audit Symposium, Paris, June 6–7, 1995.

Meyer, K., and O'Shaugnessy, K. "Organizational Design and the Performance Paradox." In R. Swedberg (ed.), *Explorations in Economic Sociology.* New York: Russell Sage Foundation, 1993.

Osborne, D., and Gaebler, T. *Reinventing Government: How the Entrepreneurial Spirit Is Transforming the Public Sector.* Reading, Mass.: Addison-Wesley, 1992.

Pawson, R., and Tilley, N. "Whither (European) Evaluation Methodology." *The International Journal of Knowledge Transfer and Utilization,* 1995, *8* (3), 20–34.

Public Management Group/Organization for Economic Coordination and Development. "Background paper to the OECD Conference on Auditing." Public Management Group/ Organization for Economic Coordination and Development Audit Symposium, Paris, June 6–7, 1995.

Rist, R. C. "Management Accountability: The Signals Sent by Auditing and Evaluation." *Journal of Public Policy,* 1989, *9* (3), 355–369.

Smith, P. "On the Unintended Consequences of Publishing Performance Data in the Public Sector." *International Journal of Public Administration,* 1995, *18,* 377–310.

Udry, J. (ed.). *The Media and Family Planning.* Chapel Hill: University of North Carolina Press, 1974.

Walker, W. E. "The Impact of General Accounting Office Program Evaluations on Government." *Evaluation and Program Planning,* 1985, pp. 359–366.

Wilson J. *Bureaucracy.* New York: Free Press, 1989.

FRANS L. LEEUW is director of the Division of Policy Evaluation at the Netherlands Court of Audit and professor, Department of Sociology, University of Utrecht, the Netherlands.

While there is wide consensus that evaluation and auditing are moving closer together, there is disagreement on the width of the remaining gap. Further integration has both advantages and disadvantages.

Auditing and Evaluation: Whither the Relationship?

Eleanor Chelimsky

In a paper written more than ten years ago, I examined some of the similarities and differences I perceived in the ways that auditors and evaluators, respectively, assess program performance; I linked these to the histories, mindsets, training, functions, and methodological approaches of the two professions and spoke to the important and promising relationships I was beginning to glimpse between performance (then called *program results*) audits and program evaluations (Chelimsky, 1985). Since that time, and based now not only on Elmer Staats's pioneering introduction of program evaluation into the U.S. General Accounting Office (GAO) in 1980, but also on a good many other experiences of collaboration between auditors and evaluators worldwide, it appears that major two-way influences are, at very least, changing the nature of both professions, even if they have not as yet produced an actual "blending of the two cultures," in Roger Brooks's phrase (1995).

Indeed, there is quite wide consensus today (and this is reflected by the articles in this volume) that audit and evaluation have moved, and are continuing to move, toward increasing closeness with regard to understanding and to methodological approach. Disagreement exists, however, about the degree of closeness that has actually been achieved, along with the reasons for the change.

Evidence from Five Observers

At one end of the spectrum, Leeuw (1995, pp. 15–16) saw the two professions as still quite different and spoke to the need "to improve the training of auditors and open their minds to the social and behavioral mechanisms operating in the public sector and in decision-making." But he also indicated that current efforts to combine "the strong points of evaluation (like the methodology applied, the attention paid to theory, and theory-driven evaluations) with the strong points of auditing (the orientation toward management, the focus on 'follow-the-money', and the attention paid to documentary evidence) may well lead to a new interdiscipline in the 21st century."

At the other end of the spectrum, Pollitt and Summa (1995, pp. 24–26) noted that "the methods and approaches of auditors and evaluators are coming closer to each other," and found only a marginal difference in the tool kits potentially available to performance auditors and evaluators. They believe this increasing closeness has occurred "as performance auditing becomes more common," and they infer that many differences in methodological approach may be more apparent than real, given that evaluators—who are typically deprived of the statutory authority of auditors—have a vested interest in laying claim to "superior methodology and expertise."

Divorski, who spoke uniquely about the differences between auditing and evaluation approaches, did not, given this topic, discuss the degree to which auditors and evaluators are moving toward each other despite these differences. Like Leeuw—that is, at the opposite pole from Pollitt and Summa—he viewed evaluation and auditing as enterprises that are still very different, especially in terms of focus and mind-set. With respect to focus, Divorski invoked auditing's need to judge whether management performance is adequate and auditors' consequent targeting of management systems and controls, as opposed to evaluation's targeting of management activities in the search to determine program results. Differences in mind-set referred to the same issue: that is, Divorski saw auditors as interested in results only insofar as they reflected management performance, whereas evaluators are interested in results for their own sake. These differences also give rise to other differences; for example, the assumption by auditors that causes for problems found can be explained via "auditors' judgment," whereas evaluators would see the cause-and-effect question as a matter for empirical inquiry. As Divorski put it: "If there are problems with results, the search is on for deficiencies in practices that may have impeded management from detecting and solving the problem." But evaluators would say that deficiencies in management practices may not be the cause of all program problems, and that improving managers' awareness may not do much to solve many of them.

Brooks (1995), somewhere in the middle of the spectrum, did not argue that the methodological approaches of auditors and evaluators are now virtually the same, but rather, from his experience at the state level in the United States, that auditors and evaluators today are "drawing upon the approach of traditional auditing as well as the approach of social science–based evaluation." Like Leeuw, Brooks recognized that "the 'two cultures' of auditing and evaluation still exist," and that "when comparing approaches across states, one observes important differences." But even though he saw these differences as real, he agreed with Pollitt and Summa that they are declining. However, he believes that the decline is "mostly because of a liberalization of traditional auditing," rather than simply the increasing presence of the performance audit. Also, he views the "emergence of a blended approach to auditing and evaluation" as a fait accompli, at least in some places.

It is, of course, difficult to generalize persuasively across the widely different institutional arrangements within which evaluators and auditors work together, and without empirical data, some of the points cited here may be impressionistic. Should we really assume that because similar tool kits are potentially available to evaluators and auditors alike, this means that the tools are equally used? Given the existence of the "two cultures," even if the methodological tool kits were identical, there would still likely be major differences made by auditors and evaluators in the application, use, and pervasiveness of the particular methods selected. (For example, I would expect to see auditors use many more surveys and case studies than, say, quasi-experimental designs, and I would also expect to see the issues of reliability—in survey questions— and of generalizability—in case study findings—handled very differently by evaluators and auditors.)

Again, if there is more "togetherness" observed between auditors and evaluators, is this due to a liberalization in traditional auditing standards and procedures? to the increasing prevalence of performance auditing? to the changing nature of policy makers' questions that force evaluators and auditors to borrow from each other? to the increased prestige of evaluation among auditors today? to the belated recognition by evaluators that auditors are right to be interested in costs? We don't really know.

Thus, although there may be little consensus as yet about how or why it has happened that evaluators and auditors, despite some real differences, are coming closer together, the important point is that many observers believe they are. And the question I would like to raise here is whether any of the mingling and blending being discussed in this volume would have happened without the physical juxtaposition of auditors and evaluators within an organization. It may well be this kind of proximity that has allowed productive comparisons of work methods and of ways to examine policy issues, to resolve technical problems, to establish credibility, such as those we see in the chapters in this volume.

It is much less frequent today than it was fifteen years ago, say, to hear "the auditor's judgment" being used as the sole basis for a finding, or to see evaluators unable to explain what savings (or expenditures) are likely to result from service changes they propose. But if physical closeness is important, then it is also important to examine what we know about how to manage auditors and evaluators together in an organization. That is, given the differences and the similarities of the two fields, and given the benefits for public policy likely to accrue from their increased collaboration, what is the organizational device that will allow us to reap the greatest rewards? Should we integrate the functions: that is, house and supervise auditors and evaluators together? Or should we keep them separate?

Separation or Integration:
Some Advantages and Disadvantages

At first glance, keeping the auditing and evaluation functions separate has a number of obvious disadvantages. Increased costs are involved in maintaining a separate group or department, and important potential diffusion-of-information benefits to the organization may be foregone unless an enlightened management takes steps to break down walls (or prevent them from rising in the first place). In addition, differences in findings among auditing and evaluation units working on the same issues but using different methods can become a problem for the organization. The normal competition between groups for organizational hegemony can move from what is stimulating and healthy to something profoundly unhealthy unless that competition is quite carefully managed.

On the other hand, separation does allow evaluators the independence they need for credibility (that very same independence for which auditors have fought so hard over their long history). Separation also gives evaluators the freedom to develop a critical mass of skills, to establish the legitimacy of their work with policy makers who may not be familiar with evaluation, and to respond to policy questions with strong studies that can demonstrate the worth of evaluation not only to policy makers but to auditors as well. Finally, one of the most important advantages of separation is its feasibility: start-up does not require behavioral change in an organization, only funds, operational know-how, and leadership.

What about integration? Most experience suggests that this can be quite difficult to achieve, at least immediately. A first problem arises because auditors and evaluators have been trained so differently, and tend to have dissimilar mind-sets with regard to a study. Auditors are taught, for example, that they are wasting the taxpayers' money if an investigation does not uncover a major problem. "If nothing is wrong," they say, "then why should we be doing an audit?" But evaluators are trained instead to ask whether some policy or program has made a difference, *any* difference, good or bad. That is, to evaluators, positive findings are as important as negative ones in improving public policy and need no special justification. To find out what works is at least as useful, evaluators think, as to find out what didn't work.

These mind-sets have some ramifications for the work process. Auditors often do their best to determine whether there is (or is not) a significant problem based, say, on a one-month informal investigation, and may then abandon the project if no significant problem has turned up. If evaluators expect that a study may generate weak or strong findings in any direction, they will often spend three months designing it (more if the policy question asked is complex or controversial), and they have difficulty in answering auditors' questions about what their findings are likely to be before they have collected their data. One result of this process is that evaluations are often afflicted by findings that are anything but conclusive, and this means that under an integrated organizational arrangement, auditors may greet the evaluators' findings with a bored "So what?" and a large yawn, whereas evaluators will always be skeptical about those exciting one-month findings that are established before data on both sides of the question could possibly have been collected.

Emphasis (or the lack of it) on measurement is another training issue that causes tensions between auditors and evaluators. The measurement questions that preoccupy evaluators (like the reliability of items in a questionnaire, or threats to the internal validity of study findings, or the real comparability of before-after or cross-sectional study data) tend to take a bit of time to resolve, are typically low on the auditors' priority list, and are usually not well understood by them. Because of this, absent training on both sides, and especially training of managers, auditors may reproach evaluators for their slowness and evaluators may reproach auditors about the validity of their findings. Unhappily, these perceptions tend to linger within an organization: they engender us-and-them mentalities, they cause morale problems, and they militate against the continuing recruitment and retention of methodologically strong evaluators whose presence is critical to the success of cross-fertilization efforts.

The point here is that when these tensions of mind-set and measurement bubble up, many of the advantages that integration was counted on to supply may not materialize. For example, in a tense atmosphere, knowledge diffusion and organizational learning may be even worse off than under separation. Differences in findings based on methodological approach are still likely to surface under integration, although at a lower level and thus more manageably—that is, easier to suppress than confront—from an organizational perspective. And even if evaluators may feel more protected institutionally than they do as part of a separate unit, the trade-off between that protection and technical quality may not seem worth it to many evaluators.

Organization for Production or for Cross-Fertilization?

Perhaps a useful way to think of separation versus integration is as a function of the institutional goals to be pursued. If the main aim is to increase the capabilities of the organization to answer complex policy questions and to begin doing that as soon as possible, then separate evaluation and audit units such as those at GAO and at the Minnesota Program Evaluation Division have much to recommend them. But if the aim is cross-fertilization in an organization, then separation, especially if it is poorly managed, may bring two important long-run costs: communication with the larger institutional entity may not be good enough, and evaluation staff may begin to feel excluded from important policy decisions.

A good example of this problem comes from the experience of the Office of Management and Budget (once known as the Bureau of the Budget, or BOB). In its early days, BOB decided to bring in people with strong technical skills to complement the work of their budget analysts, and they separated these technical staff from the budget people by creating technical centers in which the new skills would be deployed. In the words of a former BOB Assistant Director, William D. Carey, what happened was this: separation "built a kind of concentrated quality in the technical centers and it successfully accumulated a critical mass of top-flight specialists." But it also led to an organization in which technical staff became alienated. In Carey's words:

> The budget people sat at the table during the Director's reviews, but the technical people had only backbench chairs and very limited possibility to participate in the discussions. When they did speak, their comments were considered intrusive. Promotions and supergrades went to line, not staff, personnel. BOB Directors had little time or interest in the technical work, and technical staff had little or no access to them. On their side, technical people tended to look down on budget examiners as journeymen of very average capabilities [U.S. General Accounting Office, 1990, p. 23].

To remedy this developing rift within the organization, BOB decided to dissolve the technical centers and scatter their personnel across the budget divisions. In this way it was hoped that organizational cohesion and communication could be improved and that the work of the budget divisions would be enriched by the closer proximity of the technical staff's expertise. Carey believes this move to have been a mistake and its results unfortunate, for three reasons:

> First, the same problems reappeared, but at the lower, divisional level. The scattered technical staff continued to feel they were second-class citizens and now the situation was worse in that they had no organizational voice. Their sense was that they had to keep proving their worth (as technical people in a budget division) and that they were no better off in terms of having direct inputs into organizational decisions and products. Second, the professional quality of the technical staff weakened over time because the technical centers which had attracted some of the brightest people in their respective fields were no longer there. And finally, the dispersed technical personnel did not appear to have any visible effect on the work of the budget divisions [U.S. General Accounting Office, 1990, p. 24].

At the GAO and in Minnesota, where audit and evaluation units have been separate, at least some of these evils have been avoided, and certainly, with regard to visible effect, the influence of the evaluation work has been recognized and highly regarded.

In short, if integration has not been easy—and it has not—we may need to learn more about why it has been so difficult before dismissing it as an option. Is it, for example, because evaluation and auditing have different sources of credibility and legitimacy? Is it because mind-sets and cultures become entrenched under the stresses of organizational competition? Is it because we simply haven't yet developed both the management techniques and the managers needed to do the job?

My own view is that—given effective managers who know and value both auditing and evaluation, and given also some harmonization of training for auditors and evaluators—it should be possible to integrate the evaluation function successfully in audit organizations. But until that training has taken place (and especially for audit offices beginning now to incorporate evaluation into their work programs), keeping the functions separate, building multiple bridges between them, and watching their interactions and managing them carefully may be not only the most prudent but also the best organizational course of action.

A lot may be riding on this selection of the right organizational model. To be viable, both evaluation and audit functions need independence, skilled personnel, credibility, sponsors who understand the benefits to be drawn from both audits and evaluations, and the capability to respond appropriately to the policy questions of today's political environment. Such capability requires the use of both auditing and evaluation methods. When we can bring these two together and target them properly to policy makers' information needs, and when findings from both types of studies can make their way unimpeded into the policy process, then both evaluations and audits will have achieved their real public purpose: to help make government services more effective, more meaningful, more responsive, more accountable, and—last but not least—better managed.

References

Brooks, R. "Blending Two Cultures: State Legislative Auditing and Evaluation." Paper presented at the International Evaluation Conference in Vancouver, B.C., Nov. 1995.

Chelimsky, E. "Comparing and Contrasting Auditing and Evaluation: Some Notes on Their Relationship." *Evaluation Review,* 1985, 9 (4), 483–503.

Leeuw, F. L. "Auditing and Evaluation: Bridging a Gap, Worlds to Meet?" Paper presented at the International Evaluation Conference in Vancouver, B.C., Nov. 1995.

Pollitt, C., and Summa, H. "Performance Auditing: Travellers' Tales." Paper presented at the International Evaluation Conference in Vancouver, B.C., Nov. 1995.

U.S. General Accounting Office. *Diversifying and Expanding Technical Skills at GAO.* GAO/PEMD-90–18S, Vol. 2. Washington, D.C.: U.S. General Accounting Office, Apr. 1990.

ELEANOR CHELIMSKY *is an international consultant in evaluation policy and methodology and past president of the American Evaluation Association.*

INDEX

ORDERING INFORMATION

NEW DIRECTIONS FOR EVALUATION is a series of paperback books that presents the latest techniques and procedures for conducting useful evaluation studies of all types of programs. Books in the series are published quarterly in Spring, Summer, Fall, and Winter and are available for purchase by subscription as well as by single copy.

SUBSCRIPTIONS cost $61.00 for individuals (a savings of 24 percent over single-copy prices) and $96.00 for institutions, agencies, and libraries. Please do not send institutional checks for personal subscriptions. Standing orders are accepted. Prices subject to change. (For subscriptions outside of North America, add $7.00 for shipping via surface mail or $25.00 for air mail. Orders *must be prepaid* in U.S. dollars by check drawn on a U.S. bank or charged to VISA, MasterCard, or American Express.)

SINGLE COPIES cost $20.00 plus shipping (see below) when payment accompanies order. California, New Jersey, New York, and Washington, D.C., residents please include appropriate sales tax. Canadian residents add GST and any local taxes. Billed orders will be charged shipping and handling. No billed shipments to post office boxes. (Orders from outside North America *must be prepaid* in U.S. dollars by check drawn on a U.S. bank or charged to VISA, MasterCard, or American Express.)

SHIPPING (SINGLE COPIES ONLY): $10.00 and under, add $2.50; to $20.00, add $3.50; to $50.00, add $4.50; to $75.00, add $5.50; to $100.00, add $6.50; to $150.00, add $7.50; over $150.00, add $8.50.

DISCOUNTS FOR QUANTITY ORDERS are available. Please write to the address below for information.

ALL ORDERS must include either the name of an individual or an official purchase order number. Please submit your order as follows:
    Subscriptions: specify series and year subscription is to begin
    Single copies: include individual title code (such as PE59)

MAIL ALL ORDERS TO:
    Jossey-Bass Publishers
    350 Sansome Street
    San Francisco, California 94104-1342

FOR SUBSCRIPTION SALES OUTSIDE OF THE UNITED STATES, CONTACT:
    any international subscription agency or Jossey-Bass directly.

OTHER TITLES AVAILABLE IN THE
NEW DIRECTIONS FOR EVALUATION SERIES
Lois-ellin G. Datta, Editor-in-Chief

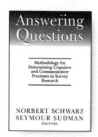
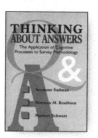